AURAS
How to See, Feel & Know

BY EMBROSEWYN TAZKUVEL

CELESTINE LIGHT MAGICK SERIES

ANGELS OF MIRACLES AND MANIFESTATION
144 Names, Sigils and Stewardships to Call the Magickal Angels
of Celestine Light

WORDS OF POWER AND TRANSFORMATION
101+ Magickal Words and Sigils of Celestine Light to Manifest Your Desires

CELESTINE LIGHT MAGICKAL SIGILS OF HEAVEN & EARTH

SECRET EARTH SERIES

INCEPTION *(BOOK 1)*
DESTINY *(BOOK 2)*

PSYCHIC AWAKENING SERIES

CLAIRVOYANCE
TELEKINESIS
DREAMS

AURAS
How to See, Feel and Know

SOUL MATE AURAS
How Find Your Soul Mate & "Happily Ever After"

UNLEASH YOUR PSYCHIC POWERS

PSYCHIC SELF DEFENSE

LOVE YOURSELF
Secret Key To Transforming Your Life

22 STEPS TO THE LIGHT OF YOUR SOUL

ORACLES OF CELESTINE LIGHT
Complete Trilogy of Genesis, Nexus & Vivus

Published by Kaleidoscope Productions
PO Box 3411; Ashland, OR 97520
www.kaleidoscope-publications.com
ISBN 978-0-938001-68-3

Cover design and book layout by Sumara Elan Love
www.3wizardz.com

Second Edition

AURAS
How to See, Feel and Know

Thai Stone Mural of Buddha with Aura Showing Around Head

EMBROSEWYN
TAZKUVEL

TABLE OF CONTENTS

INTRODUCTION

A nyone with vision out of both eyes, can begin seeing the radiating energy aura surrounding every person, usually within just 5 - 10 minutes of training, even if they are wearing glasses or contacts. That comes as a surprise to many people who assumed or have been told that seeing auras takes special psychic abilities or spiritual gifts. Having psychic prowess or spiritual oneness may help you see them in greater color quicker, but the basic ability to see auras has nothing to do with special talents. It simply requires an easy, short practice to learn how to manipulate the focusing parts of your eyes, and then to recognize what you are seeing and not ignore it.

Everything, both the living and inanimate, have auras. Energy fields of one type or another surround all living things and objects of every kind. People wonder how this can be. How can a rock or a dead leaf have an aura? It begins

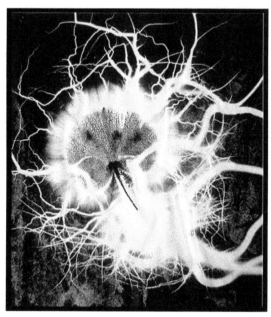

Aura of picked Geranium Leaf with Kirlian Photography.

9

with the atomic structure. Even a rock, or a deceased person, animal or plant, are still composed of atoms which are made up of protons and electrons in constant motion. This creates a very faint aura even on rocks and minerals.

Kirlian photography, which originally was only in black and white, but now is created with color, is thought by many people to produce a photographic image of auras. It was accidentally discovered in 1939 by Semyon Kirlian, and refers to a photograph made possible because of the application of high voltage in the process.

Kirlian discovered that an object resting on a photographic plate and connected to a source of high voltage would show a thin corona discharge along its edges and surfaces. Kirlian himself believed and stated that these were pictures of the auras. In Russia and Eastern European countries, these photographs are still referred to as "Kirlian Aura Photographs." But the fact that the same coronal discharge images appear when the process is applied to inanimate objects such as a coin or rocks, discounts the likelihood that these are actual pictures of the aura among scientists.

However, the scientific community was certainly intrigued by Kirlian Photography. Subsequent laboratory experiments in various labs concluded that the images are corona effects similar to those produced by a high voltage corona seen with Van de Graff generators or Tesla coils.

Another popular form of "Aura Photography" is often found at psychic fairs and produces colorful pictures that show a person engulfed in various opaque colors that extend out from the body several inches. These are also not true pictures of auras, but are made with a special camera that interprets galvanic skin responses and then adds the appropriate colors using a printer. It's like a mood ring for your whole body. Aura cameras do not use high voltage as the Kirlian method does and no direct contact with the photographic film is made.

There will be some who will argue that Kirlian photography

or the psychic fair Aura Photography really are photographs of auras. But as someone who has seen auras since my childhood, I can tell you the real thing is much more magnificent.

The colorful, ethereal, translucent fields surrounding and exuding from people that we call auras are far more complex and powerful. They are created by a combination of electrical, heat, light, electromagnetic and sound emanations from the body; and perhaps some additional as yet unquantifiable components. You probably already see, feel or otherwise sense auras around people and places you interact with and have just never realized that what you were seeing or sensing was the aura. If you have ever experienced any of these auric indicators then you have most definitely already proven you can see or sense auras:

• Have you ever come in contact with someone and feel energetically drained within just a few minutes?

• Have you ever thought of a person as a color, like he's a yellow person or she's a blue?

• Have you ever come in contact with someone and feel energized and uplifted within just a few minutes?

• Have you ever have an unreasonable fear come over you that no outward signs would indicate a reason for fear?

• Have you ever have an unexplainable happiness suddenly flood over you for no explainable reason when you meet a new person, or come into a room or a place?

• Have you ever immediately felt antagonism toward someone you have just met without knowing anything about them?

• Do you feel noticeably different just by the color or décor of a room you enter?

• Have you ever felt agitated with a strong desire to leave a room full of people, even when they may be your friends or acquaintances?

• Have you ever been with a group of people that you just didn't want to say goodbye to, even though your time for leaving was past and there wasn't anything in particular going

on in the conversation or activities to keep you there?
- Have you ever felt someone was staring at you only to look up and discover they were?
- Do you get agitated inside your skin when electrical storms are nearby?
- Have you ever been able to sense the way someone was feeling that was later proven to be contrary to the way they had been acting or speaking?
- Have you ever sensed someone nearby that no visual or audio indicators would make you aware of their presence?

Some of your reactions to the scenarios above could be from other stimuli such as body language, cultural mores, and your own psycho-physiologic makeup. More often than not, most of your feelings will stem from your aura's interaction with the people or places you are encountering.

The dawning of understanding that anyone and everyone can see human auras came as a big surprise to me when I was in my early twenties, when for the first time I looked the subject up in the library and found there were actually books written about it! I had been seeing auras in a rainbow of colors, radiating out from people like a million scintillating jewels of light, since my earliest childhood memories. Because I saw these amazing light shows on every person every day as a child, I had naively assumed that everyone else also saw them. I never really wondered in those early years why my friends either ignored me or always seemed to change the subject whenever I commented on the cool lights around people's heads.

Around eight years old I was in for a rude awakening; a shock to my innocence that pushed me far in the other direction and made me consider that perhaps I was the only person in the world that could see auras. Not wanting to think that maybe there was something physically wrong with me, I consoled myself that my weirdness was simply a mystery I was too young to understand. I pondered half in jest and half in child-like fantasy that perhaps I was really from a different planet altogether and that's why I

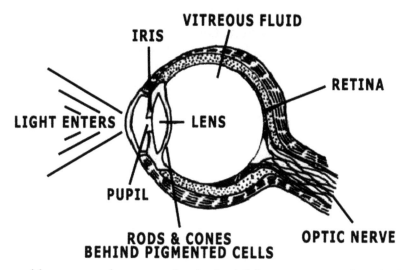

could see auras that seemed to be invisible to everyone else. As I grew older this childish fantasy morphed into simply thinking of myself as the only purple person in the world. Not black, white, yellow or red. I was purple.

By my mid-30's I had come to understand that not only was my ability to see auras not unique, but that anyone could see them with some simple training and practice. I had ascertained through reading anatomy texts and observation of myself while in aura-seeing mode, that being able to see auras was directly related to the way the eyes were focused..

Testing my theory on a few friends who universally desired to see auras but never believed they could, quickly proved the rod and cone theory correct. With just a few simple eye exercises they were easily able to see their first auras.

At the insistence of my now excited, aura-seeing friends, I began teaching public classes on how to see auras. Finding my classes always packed full of eager students I realized something more was needed to pass on the secrets of seeing auras to a wider audience.

In this book you will learn the secrets and techniques to both seeing and feeling auras on every living subject from plant to animal to human. You'll be taught the same eye exercises students in my classes learn in person. Long before you have finished the book auras will no longer be a mystery to you, as you will be both seeing and feeling them. More than that, you will have insights into what they mean that took me decades to understand.

Go in your light with love and joy,

Embrosewyn Tazkuvel

Chapter 1

I DON'T WANT SOAP
IN MY MOUTH

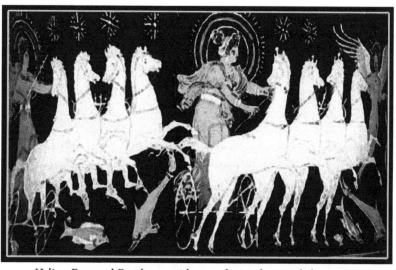

Helios, Eos, and Eosphoros with aura depicted around charioteers

It wasn't until the summer prior to the start of third grade that I thought to ask my mother what all the colored lights around people's heads meant. I was dumbfounded and uncomprehending when her answer was to tell me to stop lying and that there were not lights around people's heads. When I insisted there were wonderful, beautiful lights around her head and everyone, she told me again to stop lying or she would wash my mouth out with soap. Not enjoying that particular punishment at all, I decided it would probably be wise to not mention auras to my mother again. But she took it a step further and specifically told me to not talk about such nonsense again to anyone, as she didn't want people thinking she had a crazy son. The first fleeting realization came into my mind that perhaps everyone else really didn't see auras after all.

My mother often accused me of having the things she told me "go in one ear and out the other," and so it was with her admonition to not talk about auras. Knowing I was not supposed to talk to anyone about auras made me anxious to ask all of my friends about them as soon as we gathered that afternoon to play. I had brought the subject up with most of them individually before without much reaction. This time I had six of them gathered together when I popped the big question, "What do you think of all those cool lights around people's heads?"

Strangest thing was they all gave me blank stares like they had no idea what I was talking about. At first I thought they were joking. Then I thought perhaps they had also been threatened with having their mouths washed out with soap by their moms. Then I realized they didn't have a clue what I was talking about. If I kept asking they would begin thinking I had cooties or something, so I just laughed and told them I was kidding. And then, I never brought it up again.

Being slow to learn important life lessons in my early years, I also made the mistake when I was married at 22 years old to a very religious woman, of sharing with her my amazing experiences seeing auras. I told her about the incredibly beautiful aura that surrounded her and how seeing it made me feel closer to her. She had a different opinion of what I "thought" I was seeing. It was like my mother part deux. Instead of smiling in happiness at the compliment and wanting to know more, she looked at me like I was a visitor from Mars.

Chapter 2

THE ONLY PURPLE PERSON

Eastern Orthodox Icon showing aura halo around head

During the preceding sixteen years, until that day with my wife, I had never spoken to another person about seeing human auras, but I seldom stopped thinking about them and looking at them. They fascinated me immensely and I had continued to be captivated by their mystery. I looked at kids in school, teachers and just passer-bys on the street trying to correlate what I saw in their auras with the mood or actions they were demonstrating.

Auras came in so many colors, shades and shapes, and radiated in such an astounding explosion of tiny shards of light, it was hard to not look at them. I saw auras not just around people, but around every living thing from a dog, to a bug, to a plant. Even leaves that fell off the trees in the autumn still retained an aura for many hours, sometimes over a day, as they lay upon the ground. I even saw auras around inanimate objects though that was a little more of a challenge.

In middle school I became very interested in science and purposefully began to observe the auras around people and make written notes of how their exhibited behavior, mood or health corresponded to what I saw in their auric field. By the end of middle school I could easily see full body auric fields extending about an arms-length from all parts of someone's body. I was becoming more confident from my scientific observations that I had a good idea what the various colors, intensities, opacities and other variations indicated. The field was always most intense around the head and that was generally the area of my observations.

Though I never spoke to anyone about auras during this time, I certainly kept my ears open to listen for anyone else that might bring up the subject. But it just seemed to be one giant void. Auras were never mentioned in school, on television, in movies I watched, or books I read. I began to think I was either hallucinating, missing a few marbles, or the only person that could see auras in the whole wide world.

Whenever I looked at my own aura by standing at a distance and looking in a mirror, it had a lot of purple and white in it. Though white was not uncommon, purple was a color I rarely saw even a little in other peoples auras. At that point, beginning to believe that I might be the only person in the world that could see them, I began thinking of myself as the only purple person in the world, as a way to be comfortable with my own strangeness. Thinking of myself in this way put me at ease and took away any anxiousness about being so different from other people. Of course I was different I told myself. I was purple and the others were not, so it only stood to reason that I might have different capabilities than the world of non-purples.

Chapter 3

ON AGAIN, OFF AGAIN, ON AGAIN

Tibetan deity with aura of fire and smoke. Circa 19th century CE

As I matured into my teenage years I became more self-conscious about looking at peoples auras, to the point that I would have bouts of guilt, as if I was seeing secrets not intended for me to see. After all, nobody had a clue that I saw their auras, and that by observing them I knew if they were sick, or mad at their boyfriend, or lying to me, despite what their outward appearance and words might indicate to the contrary. If they were choosing to present a false image of themselves to me or others, what right did I have to be secretly looking at the truth without their permission or knowledge?

After years of observation I thought I had come to a basic understanding of what many of the colors, opacities, strengths of the radiating flows and other indicators meant. I knew red about the head was a very angry person getting ready to explode probably in violence, while a mellower red about the heart area often indicated someone that had turned off their rational brain and were on emotional autopilot.

I had learned years ago that seeing auras was a function of how I looked at people. I could see them or not see them with an instant change in how I focused my eyes. Just like you break a board in karate by hitting "through the board" toward a point beyond it, seeing auras merely required a focus with the eyes beyond the object being observed. It was helpful to learn how to "turn off" the aura view because increasingly during my teenage years I felt like I was snooping into people's privacy uninvited.

And there were definite perks to being able to see auras. When I was still dating, I could always see which areas women were interested in me. This gave me somewhat of an unfair advantage in our relationships. By noticing which of their energy centers they were extending out to me, and which of mine they were connecting to, I knew if they were more interested in my body, my mind, my personality, or simply attracted by the general feeling of my auric field.

I will have to admit as well that despite perks like insight into opposite sex attraction, the more I observed auras the more confused I became about what they meant. I would gain a level of confidence about the meaning of certain indicators, such as the red around the head previously mentioned. Only to be dismayed when I would see someone with the exact indicator I thought I absolutely understood the meaning of, not act in any way like the indicator said they should be acting. By the time I was a senior in high school what I thought I was seeing in an individual's aura was evidenced by their actions to be incorrect at least 30% of the time. Without reliability, I began to wonder if there was actually any useful purpose in being able to see auras.

Chapter 4

ONE IS FASCINATING, TWO IS AMAZING

Duccio's Maesta (Madonna) with Twenty Angels and Nineteen Saints showing auric halos around heads

I had never given much attention to the interaction of two or more people's auras, but in my senior year of high school with serious romances going on among many of my friends, this became a new area of interest. If you hold your arms perpendicular out from your body, the distance from the hand on one side to the hand on the other is the approximate size of the aura that surrounds a healthy body under normal conditions. But I noticed three things when a boyfriend and girlfriend approached each other. First, as they neared one another both of their auras would expand in size larger than the norm. Sometimes this expansion would grow to two to three times normal size so their auras extended a good six to ten feet from their bodies, which made their auras touch while their bodies were still twelve to twenty feet away.

Second, the closer they got to each other the more intense the light radiating from their auras would become. This was often two to three times the normal intensity of light and in some instances even more.

Third, as they embraced there would often be a rapid and dramatic change in one or more parts of their aura. Light might dim in some parts such as around their heads, and intensify around their hearts and groin areas. The colors would also change and there would be a merger of colors between the two. They each would still retain their individual colors, but they would diffuse as if they were being blended in part with the color of their partner. Areas of strong attraction such as the heart and sexual areas would begin to radiate many thin, diffused beams of white light shooting through the overall predominant color of the area, connecting one heart to another, one sexual spot to another. Once they embraced, their auras that had been expanded beyond the normal boundaries as they approached one another, now contracted to a bubble surrounding them both that was contracted tightly around them, as if they were closing out auric interaction with any other people.

I had a new fascination and spent much of my time quietly

but intently observing multiples of people interacting. Not just couples, but my teachers when they taught their class, and my friends when we were standing in a circle talking. Even the crowd in the stands at a basketball game or the athletes out on the floor with teammates and opponents.

It was very interesting to see how much auras actually fluctuated in size. Observing an increase in size became a reliable indicator for how sincerely a teacher really cared about teaching their students. If they could care less, their aura stayed the normal size around their body and their teaching presentation was boring. If they cared some, their aura would expand outward and touch the auras of students in the nearest rows. If they had a passion for what they were teaching their aura expanded outward to include everyone in the class. And it wasn't a one-way street. If the teacher's aura was expanding outward, every student whose aura was touched paid rapt attention and obviously benefited far more.

Observing the auras of crowds at sporting events also became an avid interest. While each person still retained their individual auric characteristics, a group auric field developed that expanded, contracted, and changed colors in unison. The group aura would expand to include large sections in the stands. Sometimes, such as when a winning shot was made, the entire spectator section for the scoring side would be enveloped in a singular group aura.

Most interesting was seeing two auras interact and react while the people themselves might not be having any visible notice of one another. For instance, a basketball player shooting a foul shot might be having a strong auric interaction with an opponent standing some distance away along the foul perimeter line waiting for the rebound after the shot. The two players may not even be looking at each other or noticeably communicating in any way, while their auras were having fits with each other. Even more interesting, there were often other players in between the two, and the auras of these were completely uninvolved and not having any interaction with either of the two players that were having auric confrontations.

Chapter 5

FEELING IS EASIER AND MORE ACCURATE THAN SEEING

Buddhist Bronze, Northern Wei style showing layered aura around entire body

A lot happened to me in my life between age 15 and 17. Events that ran the gamut from traumatizing to energizing and inspiring. Many events that changed my life dramatically, and even now, over 40 years later, still motivate some of my actions. One of those events was getting my first pair of prescription eyeglasses when I was in 9h grade. I got aviator style because I thought I looked cool. For a couple of days I had an extra strut to my step in school thinking I was impressing the girls by looking both scholarly and cool with my glasses. My feelings of happiness with my new glasses came to a sudden, screeching halt, when I tried to see someone's aura for the first time since I had been wearing my glasses. There was nothing! Not even the slightest hint of an aura.

At first I was sure there must be something radically wrong with that person that they had no aura at all, until I tried seeing another person's aura and they didn't have one either! I hurriedly took off my glasses like they were a caustic chemical on my face and with a deep sigh of relief to be rid of the impediment, looked confidently at another person to see their aura. Yikes! Still nothing! Seriously beginning to worry that my one claim to fame, to be the only person in the world that could see auras, was suddenly gone, I looked at person, after person, after person, trying to discern even the faintest hint of an aura. It was all for naught. I simply could no longer see auras at all.

I was beyond devastation. As much as I sometimes felt guilty about looking at people's auras and learning some of their secrets, when I could see them no more I realized I missed the ability as much as I would miss my Mom or Dad if they suddenly died.

At this point, though I understood that focusing beyond the person was the secret to seeing auras, I had no understanding about why the distant focusing actually worked. Nevertheless, I was sure my glasses were the source of the problem and never wore them or any other type of corrective lens again after that day. I consoled myself that my ability would return shortly. After all, I had only worn my glasses for a few weeks. At the longest, I should have my ability back after a few weeks to recuperate. But a week passed, then a month, then months, and my ability to see auras did not return.

For the first few weeks I was angry and in a real funk, completely frustrated by what seemed to be a devastating loss that was beyond my ability to correct. Like an alcoholic craving a drink, I desperately wanted to once again be sensitive to auras.

Bereft of sight, but intent on having something in the aura realm to cling to, I began to take more notice of feeling people's auras. It was something I had always been able to do from my earliest memories, but had rejected early in life in favor of the far more interesting technicolor show of seeing auras.

To my surprise, I soon found feeling auras actually had their own rewards when I took the time to appreciate them. There were strange and fascinating sensations as I walked by people; tinglings, heat, cold, pressure. But there was more. I could in no manner read people's thoughts, but I became very aware of somehow perceiving, through at that point means unknown, their emotional state and their feelings. Correlated with what they were speaking, and the physical sensations I felt when near them, I found to my surprise that I was able to ascertain many things about them that would be completely oblivious if I was just listening to what they were saying. It didn't take too long for me to realize I was feeling auras. I had lost my ability to see them, only to have it replaced by a wonderful new field of study.

After about six months my ability to see auras returned suddenly and completely. But during the intervening time I had been applying myself with great enthusiasm and focus to learning everything I could about feeling auras, through observation and experimentation. And the things I learned shocked me to my core.

Seeing auras had always been my comfort zone. The ability was like my best and most trusted friend. But as I stated earlier, I found my interpretations of what I was witnessing to only prove by subsequent events, to be about 70% accurate. To my utter and complete surprise I soon realized that feeling auras was actually far more accurate than seeing them on some levels. As I explain in detail in Chapter 6, the human aura is multi-layered. Each layer revels distinct characteristics of a person. Feeling was at least 90% accurate and probably more with most aspects of the aura, with the exception of being unable to zero in on health problems as is possible when looking at auras visually.

At first this would seem to be ludicrous, that what you felt was more accurate than what you saw. But aiding the overall insight, there are several other indicators that combine with the transmitted feelings to create a very accurate understanding of many aspects of a person. A very helpful visual component that was previously completely ignored when I was just observing the vivid, dancing colored lights of a visual aura, was body language, which quickly became a fascinating field of study all its own. Body language, plus the feelings in your body of physical sensations of heat, cold, pressure and tingling as you enter another person's auric field, along with the intuitive empathy with another person's true feelings, proves to be astoundingly accurate in understanding them.

Note Though in my case it caused a problem, wearing eyeglasses or contact lens has never impeded anyone else I know from seeing auras.

Chapter 6

THE SEVEN LAYERS OF THE HUMAN AURA + ONE

Spectacular 7th layer of the human aura

The human aura is the most layered and complex aura of all the living organisms upon the Earth that I have ever personally viewed. Besides domestic animals like dogs, cats, cows and horses, I've observed many animals such as bear, porcupine and deer in the wild. I've also been to zoos and looked at the auras of many other mammals including elephants and many types of primates, as well as to public aquariums where I had the opportunity to see a good variety of cetaceans including dolphins, killer whales and beluga whales. At home, I have a Scarlet Macaw and a Blue & Gold Macaw that live with me and whom I interact with everyday. I have been fascinated observing them and wild birds of all kinds since my earliest childhood. Though all of these are obviously higher life forms, as is dramatically evidenced by their multi-layered, multi-colored auras, their auras do not have as many layers or reach the intricate variance of the human aura.

The lines of the auric layers are not distinct, but I will teach you how you can view each layer separately and distinctly. Looking at them all simultaneously, there is a merging and overlapping of various layers at their margins and sometimes over their entire area. Though at first you may have a challenge separating the layers and discerning which layer is which, with practice you will be able to make slight adjustments to the way you are looking at the aura, which will enable you to more distinctly and separately see each layer.

Additionally, there is a very important eighth layer that can either be looked at first, before the other seven, or last after you have observed the other seven. This layer is composed of the balls of energy that emanate over and through the seven key energy areas of the body: the psychic center, the mind, the self, the heart, the primal, the physical and the sexual/creative.

If you try to look at the line of energy center spheres somewhere in between the other seven aura layers, or at the same time as the other seven viewed as one, the aura is just too complex to accurately discern in useful ways. It is far, far more than just

The Eighth Layer showing the 7 Energy Center Spheres
commonly known as the Chakras or Root Ki

some nebulous color blobs over the body. Many people who can see auras and see various colors in multiple locations, are likely without realizing it, to be seeing parts of the various layers. As their focus shifts by just inches, varying layers come in and out of view.

Feeling the aura, for most people, is certainly easier and more accurate for broad themes than seeing it with your eyes. But seeing it with your eyes, once you learn to separate the layers, is an entirely new world of detailed, voluminous information that can be incredibly helpful for healing.

The most effective way I have found to see the layers individually is to have someone stand about 6-8 feet away from

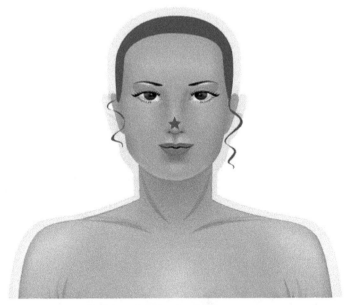

Red Star showing focal point on nose

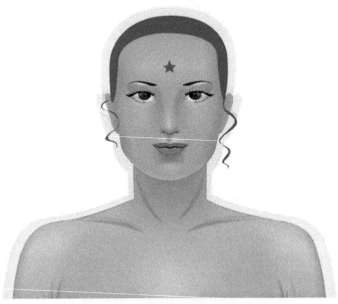

Red Star showing focal point on forehead

you, against a bare unpatterned wall, with a dull white, beige or pastel color. Stare at a single point on their face, usually on the tip of the nose, and then focus through the person, as if you were seeing and focusing on the wall right behind their head. As you learn to see auras, they will appear in layers to you as you adjust the focal point of your eyes.

If after 2-3 minutes you are still not seeing Layer 1, move your focal point up to the forehead of the person you are looking at. But remember to keep your focus at the spot on the wall behind their head.

Layer 1

The first layer, which you can easily learn to see in just 5 minutes of practice, starts out in your vision as a translucent distortion of space, like heat waves shimmering in the distance on an asphalt road on a hot summers day.

To see Layer 1, I usually focus about 6 inches behind the head. If you have any trouble focusing behind the head while still looking at a point on the face like the nose, try first focusing on the empty wall at head level. Then without losing your focus, have a person step in front of your view. You should now be directing your gaze through a spot on their face,but still have your eyes focused on the wall behind their head.

This layer is thin, usually extending only about 1 inch from the body. Except for the exception of identifying the location of physical parasites in the body, there is not much you can read from Layer 1. Other than its size, it looks the same on nearly every person that's not in the imminent moments before death or not infected with parasites. Some people will have a thicker band of distorted space which does seem to correlate to a higher level of physical vitality and energy.

As you continue to look at a person, centering on their nose but focusing on a point behind their head about 6 inches, the translucent distortion of space will morph into a translucent white or gray color making it more visible.

Layer 1 Aura

Layer 2

The second layer definitely correlates to a person's emotional state and to some extent their personality. It extends about 3-4 inches from the body and can change from one predominant color to another in a matter of minutes, just as someone's mood can change quickly. It tends to have a single predominant color which almost always is most densely colored directly over the heart area.

Viewing Layer 2 requires a focus of about 8-12 inches behind the head.

38

Layer 2 Aura

Layer 3

This layer usually extends about 4-8 inches around the head and only about an inch around the rest of the body. Normally it is larger near the top of the head and less wide toward the base. It correlates to brain activity and is one of the more fascinating parts of the aura to look at. If someone is high on drugs or alcohol instead of having a fairly uniform shape, evenly spaced from the head, the mental auric layer will have strong mountain and valley dips that move and realign frequently. The parts of the brain that are being negatively affected are obvious as there will be a strong dip in the outside surface of the mental aura layer at that point, often thinning so much it almost disappears.

If someone is having a headache it will often, but not always, show up as an agitated movement along the outer periphery of the mental layer. This is especially true if it is a very strong headache.

This layer usually is just a single color, but occasionally will have 1 or 2 other colors, usually seen as thin streaks that originate in specific parts of the head, and from that I assume the brain.

Layer 3 is most easily seen if you look through the person and

Layer 3 Aura

focus on a point 12-18 inches behind them.

Layer 4

The fourth layer extends 4-10 inches from the body, usually fairly uniform around the entire body from head to toe. Layer 4 usually pops in with a focus of about 18-20 inches behind the person.

This layer is most affected when a person reacts both emotionally and mentally to an incident. In normal mode, it is

Layer 4 Aura

often a pale yellow or another single pale pastel color, without variance or additional colors, other than a denser coloration around the heart and head area with a distinct channel of denser color flowing between the head and heart areas.

If something is affecting the person and engaging both their head and their heart, the entire fourth layer will intensify in color, particularly the parts around the head and heart and the channel between those areas. This can be from both good or bad causes. For instance, if a mother had just heard or seen that one of her children was in danger, her heart energy would greatly intensify as she felt for her child. And her mind energy would also increase dramatically as she worried about her child. This would all be very evident in the fourth layer of her aura.

Between the heart and the head is another energy center in the throat that is sensitive and reactive to a person's self-esteem and self-confidence. Because of its location between the two primary energy centers of the fourth auric layer, the throat center is very influenced if the other two energy centers start having higher than normal activity. Vise-Versa, if someone is experiencing a blow or boost to their self-confidence or self-esteem, it will often light up the head, throat and heart energy centers as well as intensify the colors of the fourth layer.

Layer 5

The fifth layer, from my experience, correlates to the physical body. This is the layer I would look at to determine a person's health, and discern particular areas of concern seen by disruptions in specific areas of their fifth auric layer, as shown by variances in color or intensity.

The fifth layer typically extends between 6-12 inches from the body. Layer 5 most often materializes if you look through the person to a point about 20-24 inches behind them.

Unless there is a malady in the extremities, it has stronger coloration over the abdomen, particularly the area of the navel, as seen from both the front and the rear. I've often thought how wonderful it would be as a medical diagnostic tool, if someone could build a machine that would clearly show this layer to any observer.

If someone is experiencing any type of sickness or injury the fifth layer will usually shrink to a smaller size, often 50% -75% less wide and the colors will darken. If they are very ill it may even shrink to only about 1 inch from their body.

On the opposite end, a person with vibrant health and great vitality will often have a width of 12-18 inches.

This is a tricky layer to interpret as it often has many components. What they all mean in conjunction with one

Layer 5 Aura

another is the test of a correct diagnosis, particularly if you are looking at a sick person and have limited medical and anatomical knowledge.

You can see a wide range of colors in the fifth layer, though usually only one to three predominant colors. If there is more than one large area of color, the multiple colors will usually be located in separate locations around the body. *Please refer to Chapter 12 to gain a greater understanding of the meaning of the colors.*

If someone is unhealthy or sick, the fifth layer will have holes, energy tumors, rips and tears over the affected area and these will be light gray to dark black, depending upon the severity of the problem. Often, if you look closely near the center of the hole or tear, you will be able to see what looks like a miniature, black funnel cloud tapering down to a point and entering the body. This is a negative energy vortex and it is pinpointing the source of the problem.

Medical Diagnosis Caution:

It is best to not try to read more into what you see in this layer than you are certain you know for a fact. For instance, if you saw a black tear in this layer over the stomach area, without anything to give you further evidence of the specific problem, it would be best to just say that you see an energy disruption over that area of the abdomen, rather than try to pinpoint which of the many organs in that area of the body was having a problem. Even if you see the tiny black funnel cloud entering the body at a specific location, unless you are certain of the organ that is below that spot, you shouldn't try to elaborate. Unless you are confident because of your knowledge, of a more detailed conclusion, for the sake of your credibility and the health of someone you are trying to help, just state what you know for sure.

Layer 6

This is a very interesting layer that I correlate to a person's core character and values. If I was going to make a snap judgment of a person I didn't know and had just met, this is the layer I would focus on. It is a big layer that extends just beyond the reach of the outstretched arms. The sixth layer tends to have a predominant color with broad streaks of other colors that may be coming from one or more energy centers of the body. These are points of influence and are significant to notice.

For instance, without yet considering the colors themselves, you may observe someone with a band of color coming from their heart center and flowing into and merging with the sixth layer. This would tell you that this person is strongly influenced in the choices they make by the feelings of their heart. This can be both good and bad and the colors would help you make the determination.

Or, you might see a broad band of color coming from the sexual center and flowing into the sixth layer. This would indicate a highly sexual person who may be prone to making choices and decisions based upon the stirring in their loins. It's quite common to see with males between 15-30. If they also had a strong color band flowing from the head into the sixth layer, as most of them do, it would let you know that though they have compelling sexual motivations they are tempered and kept in check by the rational thought of the mind. If the mind band was absent, watch out, that's a person highly motivated by lust, that will tend to act before considering or even being concerned with the consequences.

The sixth layer, both due to its size and nature, is the layer that most often interacts with the auras of other people. Your perceptions of someone are literally "colored" by how your aura interprets it's interaction with this layer of their auras. Not that other layers don't also contribute to your overall innate assessment of someone, but the sixth layer is the major contributor to that judgment.

Even if someone cannot see auras, most people do feel the sixth layer energy when they come close enough to another person to have their own sixth layer interact. First impressions

Layer 6 Aura

are most often forged by people unconsciously feeling each other's sixth layer.

It is important to note here that though you may feel negatively about someone it does not necessarily indicate that the person is a bad person in any particular way. More often, it is just showing a disharmonious meshing of your aura with theirs. (Take a look at a color wheel). Whatever the predominant color in your sixth layer is, if you take a dislike to someone for reasons unknown, and no other signs indicate they are a person with deep character flaws, it is likely their predominant sixth layer aura color is exactly the opposite of yours on the color wheel.

Most interesting about this layer is its ability to astral travel. If it is strongly connected to both your psychic energy center above your head, and to your mind energy center, plus has a smaller but balanced connection to all of your other energy centers, then this layer can expand out in one direction or another (rather than uniformly) and can travel great distances, even to the stars.

Layer 6 most easily comes into view with a focus of about 24 inches behind the person. But it can also be seen from distances up to about 10 feet once your eyes are accustomed to the necessary focus to bring it in. While training your eyes it is helpful to dial through all the earlier layers first beginning with Layer 1, then following the rest in numerical succession until you get to Layer 6. Once you are accustomed to how you need to focus your eyes to make Layer 6 appear, you will not need to go through the earlier layers first.

Layer 7

This is by far the most amazing auric level. It is never seen as a constant on a person, but only emerges at moments when they have a deep connection to their soul essence. Perhaps during an impassioned speech, a moving sermon, or while listening to music that resonates deep within them. You'll know you're in one of those moments yourself when you are so engaged with something that all the rest of the world seems to be tuned out. All of your senses, all of your heart, every thought of your mind, is only upon that one beautiful moment. During those times your aura expands and becomes a million scintillating jewels of light. At its smallest, Layer 7 extends about five feet from your body. But when you are in that blissful, natural, euphoric, impassioned state, your aura can expand to fill a room, or a town and even far beyond.

Layer 7 is actually best seen from far away. You need to be at least 10 feet away as a minimum and 50 feet or more is even better. It is rare for layer 7 to even occur, but if it does, you will be able to see it from any distance you can see the person with your normal vision. The optimum viewing distance seems to be

Layer 7 Aura

50 to 100 feet.

The first time I ever truly saw this layer was in 1981 when I attended the musical play *Saturday's Warrior* at a theater in Seattle, Washington. I had a great vantage point high up on the second level to see the entire stage. I was in the first row of the level so my line of sight was unobstructed by the heads of other theater-goers. As the play progressed I was fascinated observing the auras of all the actors and actresses as they performed and interacted with one another. The actors obviously loved their play because almost everyone's aura was bigger and more colorful than normal. There came a point where one of the female leads stood apart from the rest of the cast and sang a solo. Though I do not remember the song, I shall never forget the moment. It is seared with a delicious warmth into my heart and mind forever.

I was staring intently at the aura of the actress as she began to sing. For the first fifteen seconds or so it was larger and brighter than normal, as most of the singer's auras had been when they were performing. Suddenly it began to radiate millions of tiny, scintillating, rainbow jewels of light. My mouth gaped open in astonishment. I had never seen or imagined anything so beautiful in my wildest dreams. I was completely entranced and utterly oblivious to anyone or anything around me other than the aura of the singer illuminating the distant stage with a celestial light.

Her aura continued to expand as she sang until its outer edge was touching me up on the second level of the theater. I was surrounded by millions and millions of these tiny celestial light jewels, all emanating outward from the singer below and continuing to flow ever outward past me, to reach further and further into the theater and the hearts and souls of everyone else in the spacious room.

I noted that the jewels of light were diamond shaped with sharp edges and three dimensional in shape with eight sides, like two elongated pyramids stuck together at their bases. Rather than being a single color, each jewel seemed to have a brilliant different colored light shinning forth from each individual facet of the gem. All the colors of the rainbow and many more! More amazing, I realized the celestial light jewels were not just flowing around me, they were passing right through me, truly touching the deepest part of my soul and every fiber of my essence. I knew the same thing must be happening to every other person in the theater, even if they were unable to see the the amazing sight without eyes attuned to auras.

When the song was over I was filled with a joyous, wondrous euphoria that didn't just last for days, it has stayed with me for all of my life. All I need to do is think of that moment in time and I am transported back very clearly in my heart and mind to that joyous moment of perfect light.

I have seen the Celestial seventh layer several times since that night in 1981. The most memorable was the radiating wonder surrounding my wife when we were married under a flowered arch, next to a gurgling creek, up in the mountains of southern Oregon on a sun-filled fall day. Certainly for us, at that moment, we were the only two people in the world, and felt so light and uplifted in our auras that it seemed as if our feet were not even touching the ground.

Inside or outside, seeing the 7th layer is always a rapturous and joyful experience. Every time I see one I feel blessed. And every time it is still a wonder that fills me with peace, bliss and awe.

Energy Center Layer

The body energy system commonly known as the Chakras originated thousands of years ago in India. It is frequently bandied about these days among the enlightened of the western world, though for most, without a true understanding of its origins or the depth of the stories the energy centers have to tell. The Chakras corresponds fairly closely to the more accurate Root Ki body energy system explained in *Celestine Vibronics*. *Throughout this book the Chakra Energy centers will be referred to by the Root Ki designations of Xe, Ka, Qo, Ja, Za Wz and Vm.* In essence, both systems correctly identify 7 key energetic areas of the body.

Chakras are mentioned as psychic consciousness centers in yoga texts as early as 600 BC. The western world was first introduced to the concept of chakras and energy centers in the body with the publication in 1919 of the book The *Serpent Power*, by Arthur Avalon. This book was a translation of three important Indian texts: the *Padaka-Pancaka* from the 10th century gives descriptions of the body energy centers and practices for using them; the *Gorakshashatakam*, also from the 10th century, details instructions for meditating upon the chakras; lastly, the *Sat-*

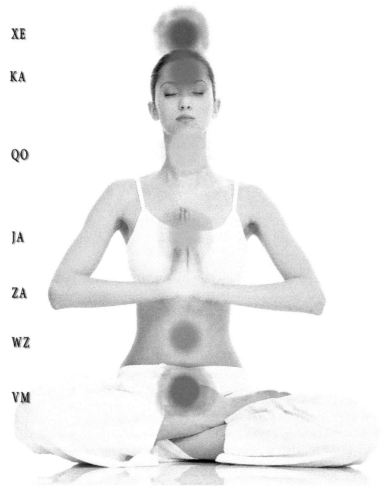

XE

KA

QO

JA

ZA

WZ

VM

Layer 8 Aura showing Root Ki / Chakra energy spheres

Cakra-Nirupana, from 1577, contains instructions from an Indian guru on use of the chakras. These texts are the foundation for modern, western understanding of the chakras as well as the basis for Kundalini yoga.

From a physiological standpoint, the 7 energy centers occur exactly over the 7 main nerve ganglia of the spinal column.

The Root Ki / Chakra Energy Center Layer is difficult to

51

assign a number to even though it is technically the eighth layer. The challenge is that some people can see this level before they are capable of seeing any of the others after Layer 1, while some people are never able to see it even after they have successfully been able to see the first 6 layers. Most people will not be able to see the Energy Center Layer until they have successfully been able to make Layer 6 pop into view. I do not know why this layer is so easy for some people and so challenging for others. I have noticed there is a great deal of what I believe may be delusional viewing of the Energy Center Layer. People really want to be able to see it, and often describe something very different than I see in both color and composition. Whether their description is imaginary, wishful, or simply a way of seeing something differently than I do, is unknown.

Part of the problem is there are many pictures and illustrations of the chakra energy centers that are published and on the Internet. These pictures always assign specific colors to each energy center respectively. Those colors assigned are far too simplistic compared to an actual aura and seldom the true color of the energy center at any particular time. The colors are not constant, but varies in size, color and density depending upon the energetic health of that area. When students claim to see one or all of these energy centers and the colors just happen to correspond to the widely available chakra charts, it calls into question the accuracy of what they are claiming to see.

The picture below shows the seven energy centers with the commonly associated colors of the Chakras. This is merely for illustrative purposes to show the locations of the energy centers. The reality is the colors, size, and opacity are almost always different. The one time the traditionally depicted colors are useful, is to visualize and call them into the corresponding energy center when you are seeking to re-balance and re-energize it.

The actual shimmering Root Ki energy center spheres are one of the most entrancing parts of the aura to observe. They are three dimensional balls of swirling energy emanating from deep in the body at their core. The size of any of the seven can vary from the size of a chicken egg to the size of a basketball. Normal size is about as big as a softball. However, they are never all the same size. For example take two people: one, who is very self-confident and spends a great deal of their time using their mind, and another who is not so self-assured and often very moved by the feelings in their heart. The former would have a big Ka (mind center) and a big Qo (throat center) but a smaller Ja (heart center). The latter would have a larger Ja, but a smaller Ka and a smaller Qo.

Their speed and direction also have wide variance. Faster speed certainly seems to correlate to greater strength in health in that energy center as long as it is not whirling ridiculously fast. The direction of the spin can also vary from clockwise, to counterclockwise to omnidirectional. Each individual is a master of their energy centers and can mentally command and visualize increasing or decreasing their size, speed and direction of spin. Doing so produces immediate energetic results.

Last but not least, the 7 Root Ki energy centers often have distinct energy cords connecting one center to one or more of the others, as well as cords connecting to them from a point outside of the auric field. This can be another person in the room or even in another city, as is explained in detail in chapters 14 and 15.

Speed, size, direction of spin, as well as color, opacity and connecting cords, all are important indicators of energetic health. As the energy goes, so the emotional, physical and mental well-being follow. Using the Root Ki energy centers to diagnose mental, physical and emotional health issues is discussed at length in chapter 16.

To be able to see the 7 Root Ki energy centers you have to not be looking at any of the other layers of the aura. This should be a fairly easy exercise if you have been progressing from viewing one layer to another as outlined in this chapter. The technique to most easily see the energy center level is quite different than the method used for the other 7 auric layers. You need to have the person stand about 8-10 feet away from you so you can easily see their entire body from head to toe. They should stand next to a dull white or light gray wall with low lighting in the room, but not too dim. You should clearly be able to see details of their clothing including color. Hold both of your hands with fingers closed together, vertically against the sides of your face near the corners of the eyes, with the tip of the thumb and tip of the forefinger touching the side of your head, and your hands protruding out from your head with the palms facing one another. It is like you are putting blinders on which allow you only to see the person directly in front of you.

Now stare directly at one of the Root Ki energy center locations on the body. Focus through the body, but not any particular

Putting on the blinders to see auras, level 7

distance. Blink your eyes as needed to maintain proper eye lubrication. Continue to stare at the location until a swirling ball of color begins to emerge. Maintain your focus for as long as it takes (usually 1-2 minutes once the ball begins to show) for the whirling energy ball to become clearer and for any energy cords connecting to other energy centers or beyond the auric field appear. Once you have any one Root Ki / Chakra energy centers in view, you will be able to immediately see all of the others by slowly moving your gaze up or down as appropriate, without losing the focal point just through the body. After you have become accustomed to focusing your eyes in the way needed to see the Root Ki energy centers, you should be able to do it in the future without using your hands as blinders.

Chapter 7

THE BODY SPEAKS

With my auric vision out of whack and inoperable I still managed to add an important visual component to my perceptions of auras by observing the body language people projected. Combined with the physical sensations I received when my aura touched theirs, the accuracy of understanding what emotions and thoughts their aura was projecting was nothing less than astounding!

Body language needs to be a book of its own and I'm sure there are many already available if you want to study the subject further. As body language pertains to understanding the hidden emotions and mental states of a person, as well as their immediate thought or intention, there are just a few that I have found are very significant and should always be noted. The interesting thing about body language is it is completely unconscious.

Similar to an aura, it tells the secrets of what people are really feeling and thinking, without them being consciously aware that their secrets are an open book to anyone that understands body language.

Multiple Verification Rule: With the exception of the handshake, a single body language indicator should never be solely relied upon. But they are great additional tools of understanding when verified by additional body language signs and visual observation or feeling of auras.

So telling is the handshake that it is the one exception to the multiple verification rule. Standing alone, the secrets it reveals about a person's personality are always accurate. Knowing this quickly revealed secret of their core personality is very helpful in understanding subsequent auric feelings or visual observations of their auric field.

The Handshake: It is common among men in western countries to shake hands when they meet. Handshakes are often given not just at first meetings, but also in business settings and even getting together with someone that you know but haven't seen for awhile. Women tend to hug more except in business settings, when they will also likely shake hands with both men and women when a group first comes together. But how everyone shakes hands is exceptionally telling about their personality.

There are five ways a handshake can occur:

1. The Limp Hand. More commonly seen with women, some men will also offer their hand totally limp without any effort to grasp or even slightly squeeze the other person's hand. This is commonly derided as the "dead fish handshake" as it is not dissimilar from holding a dead fish. Especially with men, Limp Hands are a certain telltale of a person that is not easily excitable, wants to follow a leader, and is uncomfortable and ineffective if put in any type of leadership position because they are very insecure about directing other people's activities. There is a caveat however, when you receive a limp hand from a woman. Sometimes this is a cultural training and may not be indicative of the woman's true personality. For generations most cultures and religions have taught that women should be submissive and men dominant. By presenting a limp hand to a man, as they have been taught to do culturally, a woman is acknowledging his dominance whether she realizes it or not. Some women who have been culturally attuned will present just their four fingers limply when shaking the hand of a man. That is a sure indicator that their handshake is a cultural training. But if they squeeze back at all during the handshake, even if they only give you four fingers, they cannot be classified as Limp Hands.

2. *The Bone Crusher.* Pity the poor Limp Hands when confronted with a Bone Crusher. This is a person who so strongly wants to convey their Alpha dominant personality that they will literally squeeze your hand so hard you'll think it is in a vice. If you have the audacity to squeeze back in reciprocation, they will take that as a subconscious affront to their dominance and will redouble their effort to squeeze your hand into a pulp with every ounce of strength they can muster and will usually not let go of your hand until you accept their dominance and ease off the strength of your handshake. I have seen two Bone Crushers shake each other's hand for over a minute, staring at each other's eyes without blinking, as one tries to get the other to submit to their dominance. It's hilarious to watch! Bone Crushers always want to lead. Even if they are incompetent, they can't stand to follow another person's direction. They also tend to speak louder than necessary for the same reason- they want everyone to know that they are top dog, so of course they have to do everything with more exuberance from speaking to bone crushing. Bone Crushers tend to be quite argumentative as they always want to be the person that is right. As long as you agree with them they will be your smiling friend. But if you disagree, they will talk loudly and forcefully to you presenting their side or beliefs until you either agree with them or walk away. Often times their

Figure 7-1

loud speaking is a futile attempt to assert the correctness of their position when the strength of their actual argument is deficient. Bone Crushers are very judgmental. In their opinion, you either agree with them or you are wrong. When they are put in positions of leadership they tend to be slave-driving workaholics that motivate by fear rather than inspiration.

3. Hand Angle Presented Palm Down: *(figure 7-1)* A person that presents their hand to you with their palm facing down, forcing you to meet them with your palm facing up, is a lite version of a Bone Crusher. (100% of Bone Crushers will also be severe Palm Down hand shakers). Palm down covers the other person's hand and is a sure indicator of a dominant personality, someone that likes to lead rather than follow, who has self-confidence and enjoys presenting their point of view.

The angle however, is important. If their hand is palm down and practically horizontal they will likely also be a Bone Crusher. The lesser angle the lesser dominance and need to exert dominance for them to feel their own self-worth. A forty-five degree angle is still indicating an overly dominant person that will present frictions if you oppose them. If they offer their hand with just a slight tilt to the palm down position, it is usually a sign of strong self-confidence and a person that will choose to lead if the opportunity arises. But a slight tilt also is someone you can work with that will honestly consider others opinions and not have the incessant need to always be right and the leader that the more severe angled palm down hand shakers exhibit.

These Palm Down guys are also hilarious to watch, especially when a strong angle Palm Down meets another strong angle Palm Down person. They will both present their hands to each other in the palm down position which will not allow them to shake hands because there is no way for the hands to interlock when both are in the palm down position. In these cases, one will either decide to submit to the other and accept their handshake by meeting with a palm up, or they will both mutually realize that they can't shake hands and will instead pat each other on the arm or shoulder. Remember, these are all completely unconscious actions! Palm Down individuals also tend to be fairly judgmental. The more severe the angle of the palm the more judgmental they will be. Palm Downers tend to be very ambitious and often driven by money, political or religious beliefs. In leadership positions they tend to be aggressive managers that motivate by fear rather than promise.

4.   Hand Angle Presented Palm Up: This is the opposite personality of a Palm Downer. These people hate to even be asked to lead. They can be very competent, but they simply feel more comfortable and secure following a leader. A Bone Crusher or Palm Down male will almost always be married to a Palm Up female as they would not be able to tolerate someone that didn't agree with them on everything. Palm Up people tend to be very easy to get along with and if you are looking for peace and harmony in a mate whether male or female, they are a good match. Because they do not waste any of their energy on confrontation they often times are very creative and artistic as they have more time to cultivate that part of their being. Palm up people fall into two categories in their judgmental nature.

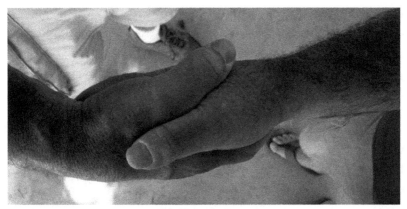

Figure 7-2

Some of them can be just as judgmental of other people and their choices as the Palm Ups. But just as many tend to be open and accepting of other people and their personal choices.

5.   *Hand Angle Presented Palm Vertical:* *(figure 7-2)* This is a straight up handshake. It angles neither to palm down or palm up. Palm Verticals tend to be self-confident, but not in any way boastful. They treat people as equals regardless of sex, race, or social standing. They are non-judgmental of other peoples choices or lifestyles and tend to have a true "live and let live" attitude. They are often very individualistic and self-reliant. Most long-term successful entrepreneurs seem to come from this group. They can make great leaders, but will also be good followers of a competent leader, but disdainful of an incompetent one. You can trust them to get the job done, whenever the need arises. If they had a preference most would prefer to be neither a leader or a follower, but just be left alone to do their own thing. If a choice needed to be made of one or the other, most would choose to be the leader, but they would lead in a much more respectful way than Palm Downs or Bone Crushers. They would strive to bring out the best in those they work with through inspiration, reward motivation and leading by example.

If you want to have a humorous but educational test of the various handshakes and the corresponding personalities, determine that you will always be a Palm Vertical hand shaker. Now enjoy the comedy when you shake anyone's hand, always offering yours to them in the Palm Vertical position.

You'll have no problem with other Palm Verticals. But when you encounter a Palm Down, they will keep their palm facing down and force you to grab it in that position. Once in the handshake position go ahead and turn your joined hands so they are in the Palm Vertical position. Palm Ups will offer you no resistance as they by nature will go with the flow. When you encounter a Palm Down, you'll have a bigger challenge. They will never turn their hand into the vertical position to meet yours. So you will be forced to grasp their hand with yours in the Palm Up position. Now comes the real fun. Once your hands are joined, exert pressure to turn your joined hands into the Palm Vertical Position. The Palm Downs will physically resist you. The more force you exert to turn your joined hands into a Palm Vertical position the more force they will use to maintain it with yours in the submissive Palm Up position. The one exception is with Palm Down shakers that only have a slight angle. They usually will allow their hand to be turned up into the vertical position and this is actually a great sign of a good leader who will also be willing to follow and assist another good leader.

Now try this exercise with a Bone Crusher and you will experience an exercise in futility. 100 out of 100 will not move their hand's position a fraction regardless of how you present yours. Nor will they allow you to turn their hand even a fraction unless you are simply stronger than they are and force the issue. Even in that case they will resist you with all their might.

Keep in mind all these actions are subconscious, which makes the comedy that much more hilarious.

The Opposite Sex Strut: This is another really funny body language to watch in action. You can witness the Opposite Sex Strut anytime a person of an opposite sex is approaching another without a crowd of people in between. A beach setting where people are wearing bathing suits and do not have clothes to hide their true body shape, is the perfect setting. Picture this — a man and a woman are approaching each other along the surf line of a beach. When they first notice each other they are about 100 feet apart and just walking in a casual slouch with their shoulders and head bent forward, probably looking frequently down at the sand as they walk. Once the two people see each other in the distance they will begin to flick their eyes up to look at one another. This will occur with greater frequency as they get closer, but they will try to do it surreptitiously so the other person doesn't notice. When they are about 30-50 feet apart they will lift their heads up and rapidly begin to straighten their spines. When they are about 10 feet apart they will both be standing quite erect, head held high, stomach sucked in and chest thrust out. The moment they pass by each other, usually within just 1-2 steps, they will quickly resume their previous slouching walk.

When this very funny ritual becomes noteworthy in regards to auras, is when you see one of the two people not do all these convolutions. If you see someone not come out of their slouch and stand erect with head high as they pass the opposite sex, it indicates someone who is very unhappy with themselves and their life, probably depressed, or they are gay and not interested in the opposite sex. If you see someone who is always walking erect, with their head held high and never goes into a slouch or changes body language as they pass the opposite sex, it indicates a very self-confident person in their physical appearance and often overly conceited about it. Even with very good looking individuals it is very unusual to not observe noticeable change in posture when walking past the opposite sex without other distractions.

The Point of Interest: This is one of the more valuable body language cues. It is simply looking at where a person's lead foot is pointing. Though this observation is accurate regardless of whether the person being observed is standing, sitting or lying down, it is most noticeable when they are standing up. Imagine three people, two men and a woman, standing close together talking with one another. Perhaps the two men have been speaking together for a few minutes and the woman has just been silently listening. From the description you would assume that the two men talking would have their focus on one another. But more often than not you would be wrong if you made that assumption. The person they are really interested in will be indicated by which person their lead foot, the foot stuck out further than the other, is pointing toward. Often if there are two men and a woman, both men will have their lead foot pointed toward the woman, even when she is not speaking in the conversation. The real fun is to observe which man the woman's lead foot is pointing toward; that will be the man she is interested in.

If you expanded to a circle of say six people, you could tell which person each of the others were interested in the most by observing who their lead foot was pointing toward. It becomes very interesting when you observe married couples and see a husband and wife talking with one another while they both have their lead foot pointing to someone else, often someone else that may be some distance away. So while their eyes may stay with the person speaking their foot gives away their true interest.

The Wandering Eye of Untruth: It is said that the "eyes are the window to the soul." If that means your eyes reveal the true intents in your deepest soul than it must be a correct adage, because they often do. It is very difficult for anyone other than a trained actor to tell a lie or even a half-truth without averting their eyes from the eyes of the person they are speaking to. Only someone that is consciously and continually reminding themselves to maintain their focus on the other person's eyes will be able to do so. The unconscious natural reaction of the body is to briefly avert the eyes at the exact moment the mouth is speaking a lie, or a half-truth or undecided about what to say. The direction the eyes are averted are also telling. However, the eyes are not as reliable of body language indicator as the handshake, so please remember the Multiple Verification Rule.

• Eyes diverted back and forth side to side are flat out lies. If the eyes are diverted to one side only it may be indicating an attempt to recall something.

• Eyes diverted upwards are a sign of someone thinking, if they are in conversation, or of boredom, if they are just listening. Sometimes it can be benign, such as when giving a lecture the presenter looks up indicating they are trying to remember something or find the best way to word what they want to present. But if it is one person speaking to another, it is more likely they are trying to think of a way to word what they want to say without getting a bad reaction from the person they are speaking to.

• Eyes diverted down is a sign of either feelings of guilt, or submission to a more dominant person. If you feel guilty when you are speaking to someone you know about something you did, you will look down at times during the conversation. The more frequently you look down the more guilty you feel. If you are speaking to someone that you consciously or subconsciously acknowledge as being more dominant than you, your eyes will flick downward while speaking to them.

However, eyes looking down at another person are a sign of dominance. Taller people have an automatic leg up in this category, but even shorter people can "look down" or "look down their nose" at taller people simply by tilting and leaning back a little with their head.

The Monkey Cue: Remember the classic 3 monkeys sitting side by side, with one covering his eyes, another his ears and the third his mouth? People do that too, much more subtly and completely unconsciously whenever they are speaking something other than the full truth. If, while you are talking to someone, or even when watching a speaker talking with a group, observe how often they touch their mouth, ears and eyes, just like the 3 monkeys. When someone is speaking a lie, a half-truth, not revealing everything, or simply very nervous talking about the subject for some reason, they will cover their mouth, (I really don't want to say this) or pull on their earlobes (I really don't want you to hear this) or wipe their eyes (I really don't want you to see this or know about it).

Some people either from reading about the subject or just observing themselves, are conscious of these involuntary actions and they make efforts to suppress them, so their body language does not give them away, but they are seldom completely successful. Instead of pulling slightly on their ear lobe they will just reach up and barely touch it. Instead of covering their mouth they will just flick their lip or the corner of their mouth with the tip of a finger. Instead of wiping their eyes they may never even get up to their eyes and just run their finger over the bottom of their nose or flick the corner of their eye with a fingertip.

A common sign of nervousness is when a person runs their hand through their hair or over the top of their head. When you see this sign you need to determine from their aura and other indicators why they are nervous. Is it because they are not speaking the truth fully, or just because being around you, or in the situation, makes them less confident?

There are other telltales when hands touch the face.

• Holding the chin in a hand unmoving or resting it on the top of the hand is a sign of boredom.

• Holding the chin in a hand while stroking it with the hand or multiple fingers is a sign of interest.

• Holding the chin in a hand while stroking it with the forefinger is a sign of disbelief.

Body language deserves an entire book of its own. The cues above are just reliable ones seen very commonly. As there can be benign meaning to each of the cues above, it is always essential to confirm a cue by seeing or feeling the aura. It is also helpful to validate body language cues with other body language cues that say the same thing.

Chapter 8

LEARNING TO FEEL YOUR OWN AURA

Auras, especially human auras, can be felt as well as seen. What may at first be invisible to your eyes until you train them, will usually be able to quickly be felt with a couple of simple exercises.

Exercise 1: Hold your hands with fingers pointing out, palms facing each other and hands spread about 1 foot apart. Close your eyes and think about feeling the space between your hands.

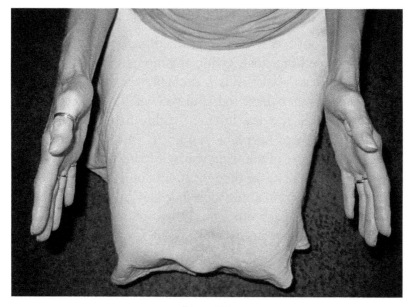

Figure 8-1

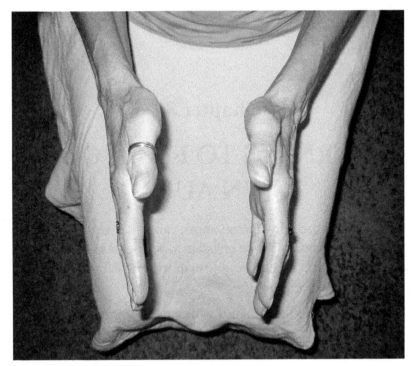

Figure 8-2

Like training your eyes to focus on something farther away while looking at something close, giving any thought to the feeling of the space between your hands is probably something you have never done or even considered. But you will be able to feel that space. Your body has the inherent ability to feel auric fields including your own. Everyone can do it. This is not a special ability, just a matter of allowing yourself to become sensitive to something you have never thought about doing before.

With your eyes remaining closed, slowly bring the palms of your hands toward each other until they are only a breath away from touching. Then slowly move them apart again. *(Figures 8-1 and 8-2)*

Repeat this action several times, in and out. You will begin to feel something as you continue to move your palms toward and away from each other. What you feel varies from person to person. Commonly, people feel a thickening of the space between the palms. Hot or cold sensations and tingling feelings are also frequently experienced.

As you repeat the action you may orient your hands in different directions while maintaining the palms parallel to each other.

If after several movements back and forth you haven't recognized any physical sensations between your palms, imagine a large rubber ball like the red ones the school children play with, being held between your hands. Now push in and out just a few inches, while picturing the squishy ball. Continue practicing until you are feeling physical sensations between your palms.

Most people will begin feeling distinct sensations with any of these physical exercises within 30 seconds to a minute.

Exercise 2: With your left arm bent at a 90 degree angle, as shown in figures 8-3 through 8-5, point your right index finger at the middle of your left upturned arm or palm, holding the tip of your right index finger about 1 inch above your left upturned arm/palm.

While remaining pointed above your left arm/palm, and with your eyes closed, begin moving your pointed, right index finger in random movements above your arm/palm.

Though your eyes are closed and your index fingertip is not touching your arm/palm you will quickly be able to feel the scribing motion of your pointed finger on the surface of your upturned arm/palm. For some people it may be as in the previous exercise, a thickening feeling, hot, cold or tingles. For many people it feels as if the tip of a lead pencil or pen is moving across their arm/palm and many are incredulous to open their eyes and see their right finger is truly not touching their left arm/palm.

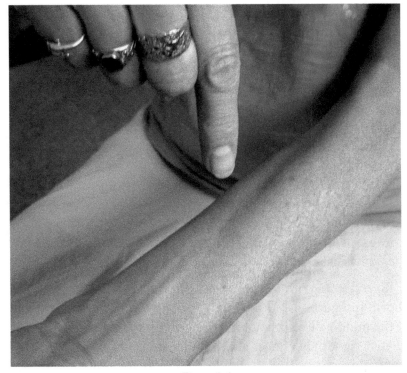

Figure 8-3

Figure 8-4

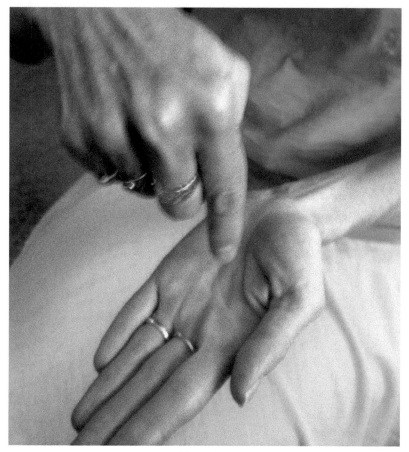

Figure 8-5

Chapter 9

LEARNING TO FEEL OTHER PEOPLE'S AURAS

Aura depicted in a Tibetan Thangka

I had always been able to feel auric fields as well as see them but paid scant attention to them until I was in my mid to late teens. Feeling simply was less interesting than seeing. As a science nerd, I loved looking at the colorful auras and correlating the peoples words and actions to what I was viewing. There were continual mysteries and surprises that held my rapt attention.

Feeling an aura frankly seemed boring. Plus, I felt that there were other factors in play such as body language when tuning into the feeling of someone's aura. But as time went on I began to notice that feeling auras and instinctively understanding what I was feeling, was a far more accurate assessment of what a person's real thoughts and feelings were at any moment, even if body language might be contributing. Seeing was far more accurate for diagnosing medical conditions. But feeling was more accurate in understanding thoughts and emotions.

Just as your palms were sensitive areas when learning how to feel your own aura, the same holds true for feeling other people's

Figure 9-1

auras.

Exercise 3: Find a partner and stand facing each other about two feet apart, as shown in figure 9-1, with your elbows close to your body, and your palms held up vertically. One person's right palm should be directly opposite the other persons left palm, separated by about 1 foot of space. Close your eyes and focus on feeling the space between your palms and the other persons. Keeping your eyes closed, move your palms slowly toward the other persons palms without actually making physical contact. Then slowly move your palms away from one another. Continue to repeat several times and note the physical sensations you feel between your palms as they move toward and away from each other.

Figure 9-2

Figure 9-3

Exercise 4: Once again partner up with another person. Have one person face away from the other, standing about 3 feet apart. The person in the front should close their eyes. *(Figure 9-2)* The person in the back should now silently make pushing movements with the right arm and upraised palm immediately followed by pulling motions with the left arm and upraised palm. The person in the front should soon begin to feel the pushing and pulling force and it is not uncommon for them to begin swaying forward and backward in unison with the invisible pulling and pushing force they are feeling.

Exercise 5: Now that you firmly recognize the physical sensations you feel when you encounter an auric field it is time to take it to the next level. Once again with a partner have one

Figure 9-4

person stand still while the other person moves around them holding their right and left arms with palms facing the standing person. Move your hands up and down and determine by feel the size of the standing person's auric field. Remember to recognize the same physical sensations you did with the smaller exercises of thickening space, hot, cold or tingling sensations. *(Figure 9-3)*

Exercise 6: In this exercise you will learn to sense what another person is feeling *(figure 9-4)*. This exercise can involve two or more people and is a particularly fun exercise to do in a group, even a large group. Make a set of 3x5 flash cards of 10 cards, with each card having a single emotion written on the card. Make a set for every person participating. Use these emotions:

1. Joy 2. Sad 3. Euphoria 4. Apprehension 5. Fear 6. Satisfied 7. Love 8. Anger 9. Jealousy 10. Compassion.

Choose one person to be the actor/actress and the other people to be the readers. Create a tally board either on a chalkboard if one is present or on a pad of paper if one is not. If there are many people in the group one person should be the facilitator rather than a participant.

Root Ki's/Chakras

The picture below is for illustrative purposes only. It shows the traditional Eastern depiction of the Chakras that many people are familiar with and the colors that are usually associated with them. However, inside each color is the name of the energy center that is used in this book, which is based upon the Root

Root Ki/Chakra energy sphere locations with Root Ki names

Ki system of Celestine Vibronics. The colors shown are not the colors you will actually see in someone's aura. For instance, just because you are looking at the Vm energy center does not mean you will see red.

For this exercise each of the participants should in unison face the actor/actress and visualize and feel their auric connections from each of their energy centers (known as Root Ki's or Chakra's). Visualize a white beam of light connecting from you to the actor/actress from your Vm (groin area) to theirs, from your Wz (navel area) to theirs, from your Za (solar plexus area) to theirs, from your Ja (heart area) to theirs, from your Qo (throat area) to theirs, from your Ka (brain area) to theirs, from your Xe (psychic center – area immediately above head) to theirs. Finally, visualize and feel their entire auric field surrounding their body (called the Oo) and see your Oo merging and intermingling with theirs.

Once everyone has completed auric connections to the actor/actress, they should sit in a single line of chairs facing away from the actor/actress who should stand about 3-4 feet behind the line, facing it.

The actor/actress or the facilitator should signal to begin and randomly choose a card from their 10 and then think and feel the emotion that is written on the card. Each of the participants should focus on using all of their senses and auric connections to determine what the actor/actress is feeling and locate that card in their deck and set it aside.

Continue in the same manner with each of the 10 emotions until all 10 have been used. The participants should be carefully placing each successive card face down on top of the previous card after they have been used, so that when completed the 10 card deck can be turned face up and the first emotion discovered will be the top card and the last emotion discovered will be the last card.

The actor/actress should also be carefully placing their cards in the same manner throughout this exercise, so when complete and their deck turned up, the top card is the first emotion they acted and felt and the bottom card is the last emotion they acted and felt.

Once everyone has turned up their deck of cards the actor/actress should come around and stand in front of them and hold up each of the emotions they acted and felt in the order that they did them. Each of the participants should make 2 piles, one correct and the other incorrect. Two to three cards correct would meet the law of averages. Four or more cards correct indicate a psychic or auric connection between the participant and the actor/actress.

Feel free to do this exercise multiple times. In my aura classes most students will get 3-4 correct their first time, but by the third time most students are up to 5-6 correct. By the fifth time, if done one after the other, many students have 7 or more correct. This is not indicating they are tuning in any better necessarily, but that they are beginning to understand and distinguish between one feeling and another on an auric level.

Chapter 10

TRAINING YOUR EYES TO SEE AURAS

A All of your life your eyes have been habituated to just a few simple ways to see things; either up close or farther away. By using a few easy exercises you can quickly train your eyes to stretch and contract in unfamiliar ways that will allow you to see auras. As a side benefit, many of my students have reported improved vision once they started doing the aura eye exercises.

Auras also incorporate more than the visible light your eyes have been accustomed to seeing your entire life. Below is a chart of the electromagnetic spectrum. Visible light is only a very

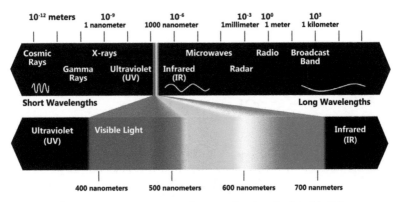

Electromagnetic Spectrum showing thin band of visible light

small part of the spectrum. As you successfully train your eyes for aura sight you will be able to see other parts of the nearby electromagnetic spectrum.

Exercise 7: Still not sure if *your eyes* have what it takes to see auras? Here's a quick, simple exercise to prove your eyes will realign in the way necessary to see auras. Hold a pencil or pen **vertically,** about 1½ to 2 feet centered in front of your face, in front of a window that looks outdoors or a distant wall in the room. Focus on the pen or pencil. Now look past the pen or pencil and focus out the window at whatever object is 10- 50 feet away like shrubbery or your next door neighbor's house. Immediately you will notice with your eyes focused to the distance the pencil that is close to your face now appears to be two pencils! Though this is an optical illusion it does prove that your eyes **will** refocus as needed to see auras. The secret of seeing auras is very simple: *observe what is close while focusing through it and upon something more distant.*

Exercise 8: Here's a similar optical illusion exercise that while only an illusion, does help train your eyes to focus in the way necessary to see auras. In this exercise, simply stare between the two short, red stripes *(figure 10-2)*. If you focus between them they will quickly multiply to appear as if there are three gray stripes or even four!

Figure 10-2

Exercise 9: The Floating Fingertips is an amazing little illusion that helps train your eyes to see auras. Sit in a short-seated chair over a carpeted floor. Turn your hands palms up, resting your forearms on your legs. Touch each of the fingers to the corresponding finger on the other hand. Now look past

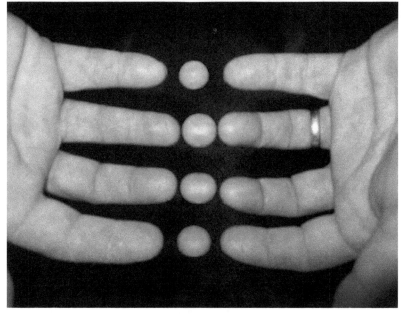

Figure 10-3

your fingers and focus your eyes on the carpet below. While maintaining your focus on the carpet, slowly pull your fingers apart about ¼ of an inch. You'll immediately notice that you now have a new set of magic fingertips floating between your fingertips on each hand! Have fun with this one. *(Figure 10-3)*

Exercise 10: Stare at the chart in figure *10*-4. Maintain a focus right at the very center of the image. Very shortly the image will appear to be moving and undulating. Maintain a focus right at the very center of the image. Very shortly the image will appear to be moving and undulating. Maintain your focus on the center and just enjoy the movement as your eyes get some fun aura-

Figure 10-4

seeing exercise.

After a bit zoom out with your focus to the outer edge. Linger but a second then zoom back in to the depths of the center black dot.

Zoom back out to the outer edge. Choose one of the white lightning bolt spirals. Starting at the outer edge, trace its shape with your eyes, following every zig and zag until you drop down into the center black hole. Now reverse it and zig zag back to the outer edge following a black lightning bolt.

Repeat these variations of this exercise to give your eyes a good workout.

Exercise 11: Now stare at the image in figure *10*-5 but don't focus on a single spot. Linger for 10 seconds or so on one spot then move to another. Soon the image will begin to change perspective as your eyes adjust to the different possibilities. One moment the right side will be an open space and the left, a box.

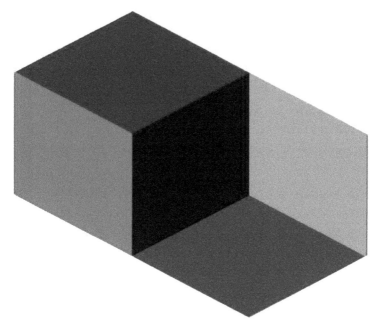

Figure 10-5

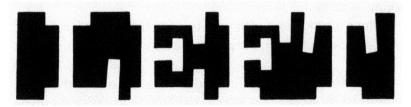

Figure 10-6

The next moment as you move your eyes they will reverse and the left side will be open and the right side a box.

Exercise 12: Look at the image in figure *10*-6. It clearly spells a four letter word. Once you see it, look away, then in a few moments look back. With just moments of practice and your eyes should begin readjusting in seconds to see the image.

Exercise 13: Beginning at the outer point trace the square spiral pattern of the black line in figure *10*-7 with your eyes all the way to the center. Once at the center, retrace the route back to the outer tip with your eyes following the white line.

Now follow the black line back down to the center. Once there just stare at the center spot. Hold your gaze until the image begins to change from a flat picture to a three dimensional pyramid projecting up to an inverted pyramid dropping down. If the image does not switch back and forth from in to out fairly quickly, then just move your focus a bit to another part of the image and then back to the center. Repeat until you achieve the 3D affect.

Exercise 14: Look at figure *10*-8 and think of it as a framed star window. You can look through it to the space beyond. Practice looking through it then zooming back to see it framed in the black. Then zoom through it to see the white space beyond. As you exercise your eyes, the image will become three dimensional and holographic seeming to be floating above the image.

Exercise 15: Ready for the super whammy? The chart in figure *10*-9 has several valuable elements. It is a serious exercise for your

Figure 10-7

eyes. Start at the outer end and follow a band all the way around until you are back where you started. Drop down to the next line and repeat. Continue in this manner until you reach the center and drop your focus through the small black square. Now backtrack and repeat the procedure until you are back on the outer band. Once more drop band by band down to the center. Now just hold your gaze on the small center black square. You should begin to see undulations and 3D effects.

Next quickly zoom in and out with your focus from the center black square to the outer bands and back to the center again. Do it dozens of times in a single minute..

Larger images are more effective training tools for aura eye

Figure 10-8

exercises because they force your eyes to move over greater distance, which further extends the focus range of your eyes. To help overcome the size limitations as of a printed book, all of the eye exercises are also located at www.celestopea.com/eye-exercises.html. If you view them on your computer they will appear as large as your monitor allows, as well as in color.

Exercise 16: With more than a dozen aura eye exercises under your belt you have certainly begun to add new dimensions to the aura-seeing abilities in your eyes. You are ready to start learning to see the first layer of the aura by looking for your own.

In this exercise *(figure 10-10)* simply put your hand with

Figure 10-9

fingers splayed apart, against an off-white or lightly colored wall in a room with a normal level of natural or artificial light. Look at your hand, but focus through it to the wall beyond. Now slowly move your hand up and down a few inches either direction. Within a couple of minutes, often within just a few seconds, you will begin to see the first layer of the aura with the translucent, distorted space close to your hand and in between your fingers.

Exercise 17: This is a similar exercise as the previous, but using your feet instead of your hands. *(figure 10-11)* You can do this against any background, but it works easiest if the background is a bare off-white or light colored wall. In the morning when you

91

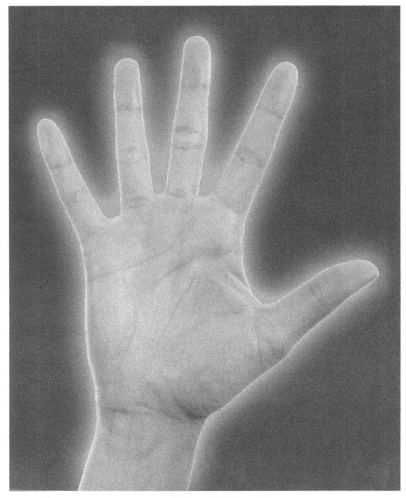

Figure 10-10

first wake up stick the ends of your feet out of the bed covers. In the same manner as the exercise with your hands, look at your feet but focus to a point just beyond them. You will soon see the translucent distorted space of Aura Layer 1 all around the periphery of your exposed feet.

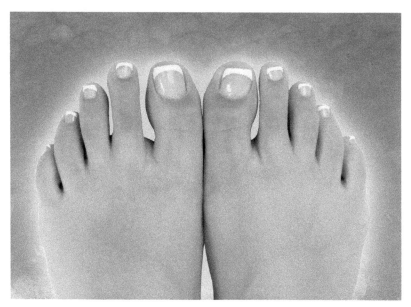

Figure 10-11

Chapter 11

AMAZING, ASTOUNDING, INCREDIBLE TRAINING TOOL

The invention of Magiceye 3D pictures created the single most effective tool for learning to see auras. When your eyes refocus in the manner necessary to see the 3D image you have just used your eyes in the exact manner necessary to begin seeing auras. When you see a 3D picture you are looking at something that is close, but your eyes are focusing on something that is farther away, beyond the object you are actually looking at. That is the exact technique for seeing auras. Although there are many other eye exercises you can do to help train your eyes, including some in this book, all of them pale compared to Magiceye 3D pictures. I cannot emphasize enough that doing your eye exercises with the Magiceye 3D pictures will help you not only see auras quickly, it will help you see them in vivid colors and far greater detail than any other method you employ in your training. If you do no other eye exercise except learn to see Magiceye 3D pictures within an instant of looking at them, you will be well on your way to becoming very proficient at seeing auras in full, vibrant color.

Time after time in "How to See Aura" classes I have taught, there would always be students who struggled to see more than the thin opaque white auric outline after concluding the basic eye exercises. But once they successfully could zoom in to the

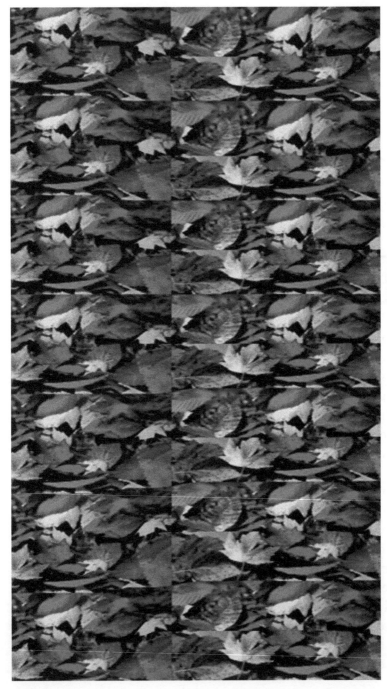

Magiceye 3D pictures, they immediately began to see auras in wispy, pale colors and the world of seeing auras truly began to open for them.

An Internet search for Magiceye 3D pictures will find several sites where you can view a wide variety of Magiceye 3D pictures. Here are internet addresses of a few good ones:

www.magiceye.com

www.magiceye3ds.com/pictures.aspx?page=1

www.vision3d.com/sghidden.html

If you truly want to see auras in fullness and in vivid color, please visit these sites and incorporate viewing and seeing Magiceye 3D pictures for at least 15 minutes each day. This is the fastest method to train your eyes to see auras. With some people, one 15 minute session is all they need. Other people may need several sessions before auras are seen in color and fullness. Persist until you succeed. As long as you have vision in both eyes, even if it's terrible vision, you will succeed if you persist. The longest I've known someone to persist until they achieved success is 16 fifteen minute sessions. So even if it's challenging for you it should not take that long before you are having great success seeing auras.

You should know that your eyes will not be damaged by viewing Magic 3D pictures. In fact, just the opposite, as eye specialists use Magic Eye 3D pictures for vision therapy. Think of viewing Magic 3D pictures as Zumba for the eyes.

If you are viewing the Magic 3D pictures on your computer, to insure eye safety, maintain a normal distance from your monitor screen and remember to blink normally.

In addition to helping you be able to see auras, according to the Magic Eye websites, Magic Eye 3D pictures are also useful for "improving vision, relaxing the body and calming the mind."

To have the Magic Eye 3D picture "pop" into view simply focus through the picture. You can do this most easily by picking a single, tiny spot near the center of the image and from a distance of a foot to two feet, focus solely on that spot. Fairly quickly the 3D picture should pop out. Once the 3D picture becomes visible the longer you look at it the sharper the image will become. Once it is in focus you'll be able to move about in the picture, viewing different aspects and locations.

Chapter 12

UNDERSTANDING THE
MEANING OF WHAT YOU SEE

Virgin of the Immaculate Conception and son, showing aura around heads

There is no easy answer to that question. Colors can have various meanings depending upon what part of the body is being observed, what the auric field feels like overall, what the body language is saying, and what effect the surrounding area or circumstances may be having on the person. You should never make a judgment based solely on the color showing in a particular part of the aura. Depending upon what they are indicating, many colors can change quickly as well. You may look at a person one moment and see red around their head, then look at them again a few minutes later and see the red has become yellow or some other color.

With the understanding that color alone cannot be used to make judgments or diagnosis, and that the location and other factors also have to be taken into account, here are some general guidelines for colors in an aura.

Pale colors of various hues: People just learning to see auras will see pale colors before they learn to see vivid ones. If this is where you are in your aura-seeing progression then the pale colors have no relevance. If you are to the point that you can see vivid colors and a part of the aura is showing pale colors rather than the vivid colors seen elsewhere, then you are seeing an area of weakness. The location and other telltales, including cords, within the person's aura from one energy center to another must all be taken into account to determine what the cause of the weakness is – mental, emotional or physical. If it is mental, there will be a cord from the pale area to the Ka (head). If it is emotional, there will be a cord from the heart area to the pale area. If it is physical, there will be a cord from the pale area to the Wz energy center. There may be more than one cord to various energy centers and there may be a cord traveling out of the aura to someone unseen. All indicators must be taken into account together to solve the puzzle of not only where the problem lies, but more importantly, what the root cause of the weak area is.

Translucent black and gray: These are also always signs of auric weakness, unless upon rare occasion you encounter a person whose entire aura is translucent black or gray. If you ever encounter such a person, run the other way. For your own safety, have absolutely nothing to do with that person, even the simplest of conversations. For one reason or another they are a very negative energy, always with either a perverted connection to their own heart or no connection at all. Their mind connections are always convoluted and often disconnected as well. They may be having just a temporary bad trip on drugs or idiocy from alcohol, or they may be a sociopath or worse.

If you are only seeing splotches of black or gray they are merely indicating areas of weakness in the auric field, which like the pale colors could be of a physical, mental, or emotional nature. Again, pinpoint the problem by observing other indicators, especially energy cords running from the problem area to specific energy centers of the body.

When a black area seems to be almost alive, moving frequently within a specified area that may be as small as your fist or as big as a person's head, this is indicating there is a negative energy or entity that is physically attached to the person's auric field and feeding off of their energy. A normal auric weakness will have a black or gray area, but it will not be moving about energetically, with a clear defined outer boundary. Regardless of your beliefs, these are real energies which you will clearly and frequently see on people as you develop your ability to see auras. These are so common that about half the people you encounter will have one to four negative entities attached to their auric field. A bad case would be three to five. I have counted as many as twenty on one person. The negatives entities are quickly dispatched using the same techniques with a wand or crystal used to remove negative energy cords.

White, either solid or translucent: This is the most commonly seen color in an aura and the first color most people see around someone's head when they are first training their eyes to see auras. A strong component of the aura is light. White light is actually the color that is created when all the colors are combined. Think of a rainbow which separates all the colors of the white sunlight because of the prism effect of misting rain. Put all the colors back together and once again you have white light. When you are first learning to see an aura your eyes are not yet sufficiently practiced to separate the colors so all you see is white or translucent white or clear like heat waves on a road. As you continue to exercise your eyes you will be able to separate the colors of the white light just like a prism does with sunlight.

Though auras may have large blotches of color such as yellow, purple, blue, red and green, the overwhelming aspect is the millions of multi-colored, jewel-like shards of light streaming out of the aura in every direction. However, though this is a constant state of an aura, a person very rarely has sufficient passion about the moment to project it vivid enough to be seen, except in exceptional circumstances. But it is because of this beautiful rainbow aspect of the aura that you initially just see white or translucent shimmers when you are first learning to see auras.

Brown: This is a color seldom seen but it also indicates a problem in some part of the body. You need to determine from other indicators whether it is rooted in emotion, mental or physical causes, or multiple sources. When you see brown rather than black or gray it usually seems to depict a problem that has been existing for quite a while. When you do encounter brown, it is not uncommon to see it laying under a layer of translucent black.

Red: Red tends to mean either anger or passion, depending upon where it is located. If it is around the Ka it is almost always anger. Around the Ja or Vm it is always passion. If it is around both the Ja and Ka it shows an angry passion such as jealousy. When you encounter red it is very helpful to observe the other indicators, particularly body language to ascertain the source of the energy causing the red to manifest. Red is often fleeting and can disappear quite quickly to be replaced by other colors.

Opaque colors: Aura colors are almost always of a see-through translucency. Occasionally you will encounter a denser more opaque color in part or all of the auric field. This often indicates someone that is closing out interaction with other people for one reason or another. They may still talk to others, although they are more likely, even in socializing, to be withdrawn. When you encounter opaque colors the other indicators are essential to determining why that person's aura or part of their aura is opaque. What is their body language saying? What does their aura feel like? What are their actions evidencing? What cords do you see? Where are the cords going or coming from? If you see red in the head area coupled with opaque colors this is very likely an angry person, holding their anger in and plotting something that will hurt one or more people in some way in a very short period of time.

Yellow: Next to white, yellow is the most commonly seen color. It is usually the first color noticed after white/translucent that a person's eyes adjust to seeing when they are learning to see auras. After you are proficient in seeing the vivid colors, encountering yellow takes on more meaning. If it is over the Ka and/or Ja it is indicating a mellow, open-minded person who does not get easily riled, but also does not get passionately excited very easily. If it is over one of the other energy centers, it is usually a simple indicator of everything being harmonious in that area at that time.

Blue: Blue comes in several shades from sky blue to deep blue. The lighter shades are more commonly encountered and the darker shades quite rarely. Blue is most often found over the Xe and indicates someone in whom spirituality and/or psychic abilities play an important part in their life. It is sometimes found over the Qo and shows a person of conviction that will not be easily swayed to a different opinion.

Green: Is a fun color to see on people. Regardless of which energy centers you see it over, these are people that are enthusiastic and optimistic about their lives or projects they are working on.

Pink: Is a very forgiving person. The color is almost always found over the Ka and Ja when it is present. It is often also seen over the Qo and Vm.

Purple/Violet: This color is most often encountered over the Xe with the second greatest frequency being over the Ja. It indicates a very spiritual person, though they may not be religious. If it is the strongest over the Xe, it is a person very open to discovering and utilizing their psychic gifts. On rare occasions you will find it around the Za energy center and this will indicate a person that has strong connections to past lives, which may be their own or other peoples. They will often be ardent students of some historical time or culture. There is a downside to this color, which is some people showing purple/violet can become obsessed with their psychic abilities or historical area of research, to the point that the purple/violet color predominates their entire aura, leading to a very one-dimensional personality.

Aura almost all one color: This is never a good sign when you see it unless you are just looking at a single layer that is usually just a single color. The mono color itself can be a wonderful one such as the purple/violet just mentioned. But there are 7 major layers to an auric field each with their own unique aspects and colors. If any color dominates the entire auric field it indicates a very unbalanced personality. Not crazy unbalanced, but too fixated on one aspect of their life to the detriment of all the other areas. For instance, you may see red as an auric field dominating color and see out-flowing cords emanating from the Vm to some or all of the other energy centers. This is showing a person whose life revolves around sex, and almost all of their choices of what to do with their time will in one way or the other be related to sex. Other aspects of their life such as developing relationships not based upon sex, or expanding their knowledge of subjects not related to sex, simply hold no interest for them. Or perhaps you see green, another usually very favorable color, predominating the entire auric field with out-flowing cords from the Ka to many of the other energy centers. This indicates a person who has a great intellectual excitement (and passion if mixed with red) about some subject. They are so interested in their mental pursuit and thirst for knowledge about the subject that they neglect other areas of their lives.

In extreme cases, people with mono color auras can have a lot of physical ailments from malnutrition to illnesses simply because paying attention to the state of their body has become an afterthought to their lives, if they think of it at all.

Turquoise: This is an interesting and unusual color to encounter. Just like mixing paint it seems to convey all the energies of both green and blue. I have always found people with turquoise in one or more energy centers to be very balanced people, with high standards in their life, excitement and enthusiasm for what they are pursuing and interested in, and a desire to truly grow and expand themselves during their lives. They all seem to know that they, as a person and as humans, are much more than we imagine. They are ever in pursuit of discovering and embodying those ethereal calls to greatness.

Chapter 13

STAGES OF PERCEPTION PROGRESSION

This is a guide to what you are seeing visually in a human aura. It is based upon over 50 years of personal observation and correlation with observed actions and conditions. Please do not accept these explanations as 100% accurate unless you verify them with one or more other corroborating signs such as body language, visible symptoms, known facts, and how the aura feels to you. In addition to what you see and know, you have great empathetic powers; use them!

As you begin to look at people's auras you may want to start with family and friends in your home. The easiest place to see an aura is around someone's head and it's best to have them stand near a dull white wall in normal indoor room light. Do not focus on their face, but look through them as if you were focusing on a point on the wall directly behind their head. At first you will just see Layer 1 as a translucent distortion of the space around their head, kind of like heat waves on a blacktop road on a hot summers day. But there will be no doubt that you are seeing something you have never seen before!

From there, just begin to practice with the additional techniques and exercises in this book and if you are like most people you will begin to see auras in a rainbow of colors. With continued practice you someday should be able to see auras in their full magnificence and there is truly nothing like it that you can imagine or compare. Prepare for the experience of a lifetime the first time you see the million scintillating jewels of color radiating out from the body in Layer 7, forming rainbow connections to other people, animals and plants. Truly, seeing auras is one of the most fascinating and rewarding skills you will ever learn.

What you can identify depends upon what you are seeing

There are distinct stages which people go through as they gain the ability to adjust the focus in their eyes to see auras. Occasionally someone may be able to zip through the stages in a matter of a few hours of very focused effort. More often it will take 6-12 hours of focused eye exercises, spread out over multiple days or weeks to reach the point where you can see human auras in vivid color and with great detail. However, the vast majority of people, if they have vision in both eyes, will usually be able to see the first stage of auras in less than five minutes! This rapid gain of a heretofore unknown ability, usually encourages people enough that they will continue their eye exercise until they can see the first faint, pale colors, then the vivid colors and lastly the great detail. As auras occur in 7 distinct layers plus the Energy Sphere layer, when you are first learning to see them there will often be an overlapping meld of multiple layers making for some interesting colors. Here are the stages most people go through as they learn to see auras:

Stage One: Translucent disturbed space within six inches of the human body becomes visible. This looks somewhat like heat waves on a hot highway. It is most easily seen around the head, with the person that is being viewed standing against a white or near-white wall with normal daylight or interior lighting, and the viewer standing five to ten feet away.

Though it is exciting to be seeing your first auric fields, you are not seeing enough at this stage to make any conclusions about the person you are observing.

Stage Two: Same as Stage One except the aura will likely be seen six to eight inches away from the head and very pale colors will begin to be seen. Yellow is usually one of the first colors noticed and lighter colors will more likely be seen than darker colors. The one exception is black, which may be noticed as a translucent color in certain areas of the body if the aura is being observed around the body and not just around the head.

Congratulations! By seeing your first pale colors and a larger auric field you have moved up to Stage Two. However, there is still too little seen to give you any helpful information about the person you are observing. Keep up your eye exercises and gain the next stage.

Stage Three: The Stage One disturbed space, heat wave type aura will be seen three dimensionally all around the body. It is easily seen from the head to the toes viewing from the front, back or side. Additionally, a wide range of pale colors will become visible, often coming and then vanishing, then reappearing, and swirling with other colors. Faint translucent lines of surging power will be able to be discerned running through the auric field connecting the Alpha/Omega Gateway points, which are the top of the head, the palms of the hands, and the soles of the feet. You may not yet see the full connecting line running from one gateway to another, but may only see the power cords emanating from each of the gateways, but then becoming invisible a short distance later.

This is the first stage where you can begin to make some limited conclusions about the person you are observing based upon the wide range of pale colors you are seeing.

Also, if you notice a weakness in the auric field, an area where it is depressed inward and not visible as far out from the body as the overall auric field, you can know that there is a problem in this energy center area. The area it is located in will give you a hint as to the possible problem. For instance, an inward depression in the heart area tells you there is a problem with the heart. But you will need additional information from other observations and knowledge to determine whether it is something like an

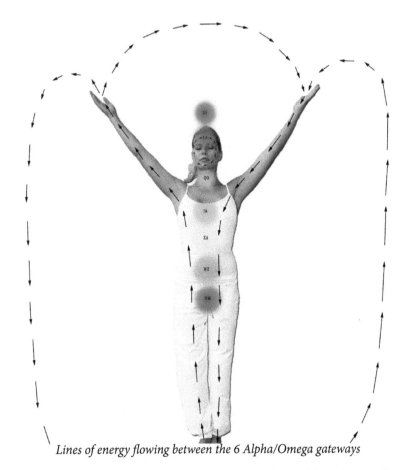

Lines of energy flowing between the 6 Alpha/Omega gateways

emotional problem stemming from something like relationship challenges, or a physical problem, stemming from something like cardiovascular disease.

Also, the color translucent black in any area indicates a problem or energy blockage. Again, you will need additional information from other sources to pinpoint the problem. If the translucent black is also in an area of inward depressed aura it is often a sign of a fairly serious problem.

Stage Four: The aura colors will become very vivid in most places and will be clearly seen over the body in addition to the periphery. You should be able to faintly begin separating the 7 main layers as outlined in Chapter 6. Remaining pale colors that you see are pale for a reason other than your ability to view the aura. In addition to the Alpha/Omega Gateway power cords, you will begin to see an overall radiating out effect of the auric field, distinctly showing the power source as the human body. Additionally, you will notice pale, translucent power cords coming in from outside the auric field and attaching to various points on the auric field over one or more of the Root Ki energy center areas. There may be one or two of these cords or several dozen. Some may connect to other people in the room, in which case you will be able to follow them to their opposite connecting point. Others will be seen to be exiting the building through the walls, roof or floor and traveling to points beyond unknown.

Stage Five: The overall aura becomes intense. You will easily be able to separate the 7 main layers of the aura and look at each one distinctly. If you are in a situation that you can see Layer 7, it will appear as a radiating jewel of millions of tiny shard-like reflections of rainbow colored light emanating out from the body. Though certain areas can have a predominance of one or more colors, the overall effect is like looking at millions of tiny, scintillating jewels, densely packed together and shooting out in all directions from the body, fading into invisibility as they near the edge of the visible auric field. It is a breath-taking and unforgettable sight the first time you see it. Even after all the years I have looked at auras, I still find myself catching my breath in awe and wonder whenever I have the rare opportunity to see this astounding light show of energy.

There should be a perfect symmetry to the overall aura shape. Any areas that do not project out as far are showing a weakness in that area of the body.

Once you have reached Stage Five and any of your open-minded friends, family and acquaintances know about it, you will likely often be asked to look at their auras and tell them what you see. Many times what you see will not be a pretty sight and it is most often difficult to tell them the truth. For those that can bear both the good and the bad, you can help them tremendously with any of their energy issues, because in seeing the aura you also have the ability to affect it, both beneficially and detrimentally.

Chapter 14

CORDS OF POSITIVE, NEGATIVE & RECIPROCATING ENERGY

In Stage Five, cords of highly active energy connecting areas of the body as well as connecting to other people and areas outside the body are very evident. These cords, especially if they are transiting the auric field to some other person, can highly influence a person's physical, emotional and mental health, both beneficially and detrimentally. The direction of their flow and their color, immediately show whether they are positive or negative cords.

Your first clue as to the whether a cord coming into or exiting the auric field, is beneficial or detrimental, is the direction of the energy flow. If the energy is flowing one way out from the person through their auric field to a point beyond, it is most likely connecting to another person in a dominant, often overbearing or stifling way. If this is the case, the color of the cord will be in darker tones. Occasionally, an outward flowing cord may be beneficial, such as a mother's cord to one of her young children. If it is a beneficial cord it will show up in lighter colors. Beneficial cords can be a myriad of lighter colors, while detrimental cords always have a darkness about them.

A cord showing a one way inward energy flow coming from an unseen point beyond the auric field is most often a negative cord. If it is also dark in color, it is showing a dominant energy coming into the person from someone else. Occasionally you will see a lighter colored, inward flowing, beneficial cord, but it is quite rare in adults.

The cord you should look forward to seeing is one where there is energy flowing both directions, both in and out. These will always be lighter in color and show a mutually beneficial reciprocal energy exchange between the person you are looking at and someone else beyond their auric field.

Every cord will terminate at a specific location on the body correlating to one of the spherical Root Ki Energy Centers. Typically, a person will have several cords, coming in and out of multiple energy spheres and often from more than one person beyond their auric field.

Energy cords will also be various diameters. Some will be as big as six inches in diameter and very obvious. Others may be smaller, down to mere tendrils that are barely visible. Typically, major cords are about two inches in diameter.

You can also see smaller, secondary cords going from one Root Ki Energy Sphere to another. If they are connected to an incoming or outgoing cord transiting through the auric field from another energy center, they will exactly match the color of that cord and show one energy center affecting another because of the transiting cord. If they are a cord only connecting one energy center to another within the person's own auric field, and not connecting to another person, the color will be different from any cord transiting the auric field.

Along with the color, observing where cords go or terminate is very helpful in making a diagnosis about any problems. For instance, you might notice a weakness in a person's aura near their Vm center. This is the center of sexuality and creativity located in the crotch area. You may also notice a darker cord entering or leaving the Vm area. Where and how it terminates tells you an immense amount about the problem. If it terminates in the person's Wz area, the location of their energy sphere of the physical, and has a reciprocal movement, then the problem in the Vm is of a purely physical nature like an infection caused by untimely exposure to germs, or a muscle strain caused by over exertion.

If the cord terminates in the persons Ja area, the seat of their emotions, and the energy flow is from the Ja to the Vm, then the problem is obviously emotional. The Vm area may be experiencing physical problems such as a bladder infection, but this is being induced by emotional upset in the Ja that has weakened the persons resistance to infection.

Likewise, you may see the cord terminating in the Ka area, the location of the mind. If the energy flow is from the Ka to the Vm, then the cause of the Vm's problems are rooted in the mind, such as anxiety about finances or relationships. Solve those problems and the Vm will be restored to good health.

Terminations of major cords in the Ka, especially if the energy is flowing out from the Ka, will almost always also have smaller cords from the Ka to other areas or people. For instance, a bladder infection, instigated by their Ka because they are anxious about a relationship, will likely show two smaller cords leaving the Ka, one going to the person's Ja, because they are also emotionally upset, and another going out into space, connecting at a point unseen with the person with whom they are encountering the relationship challenge.

You have to be very cognizant of any cords leaving the person and vanishing into the distance to a person unseen, and even more aware of cords coming into the person from another unknown person beyond your sight. It is really amazing how many problems people have physically that are caused by negative energy connections to another person, from a lover to a co-worker, to a teacher, a friend, a parent, a child, or a boss.

When you see a cord going out from a person it is important to notice if there is another cord laying right on top of it or intertwined with it coming in. For some reason I see a lot of women with negative incoming connections from men, where the women still are drawn to the man despite the negative energy they receive from him. If this were the case, the outgoing cord from her to him would be a lighter color, perhaps with a few

115

moving dark blotches indicating her upset with the relationship. His incoming cord to her however would have a uniform darkness, or a darkness with just a few moving blotches of light, showing he still had a few good desires. More often, in non-reciprocal cord connections, the man's cord coming in is just dark. His dark energy is pulling the woman down, while the light energy she still gives him continues to buoy him up.

If this were a healthy and mutually beneficial relationship, there would only be a single, reciprocal, lighter colored cord with synergistic energy flowing both directions.

You can tell the depth of a harmonious relationship by the thickness of the light colored cords and the luminous energy emanating from them.

You can also know with a fairly good certainty if a relationship will endure by how many energy centers connect between the two people. Have a couple stand facing each other about 6 feet apart and observe the cords that connect them between Root Ki Energy Spheres. Oftentimes, especially with young love, there are only connections between the Vm's and the Ja's, the sexual areas and the hearts. Those types of relationships almost always burn out because they have no substance or common areas of harmony and interest.

Another thing often and sadly observed between men and women is they have two completely different takes on each other and this is blatantly obvious in the cords that connect them. It is very common, especially with people between the ages of 15 and 35, to see a woman sending powerful cords to the man's Ja and Vm, while the man has no reciprocity at all with her cord to his heart and does not return one to her. His one and only cord is to her Vm, and sex is the one and only thing he is interested in despite what he may be trying to convince her of with his words or outward actions.

Chapter 15

CUTTING AND HEALING THE ENERGY CORDS

If someone is experiencing any mental, physical or emotional problems that are being caused or exacerbated by negative cords, they must be permanently removed if there is going to be a permanent healing. If this is not done, even if they go to a doctor and think they have the problem solved, it will re-manifest again in the not too distant future, sometimes as the same physical malady and sometimes a different one. But it will never go away for good until the negative cords are cut.

There are multiple ways to remove negative cords. If it is an internal cord, one that is completely inside the persons own aura, such as a cord from the Vm to the Ka, it is useless to remove it by force, because the underlying root cause will still remain and the cord will quickly regenerate. The underlying cause must be determined by following the energetic clues, and that cause must be remedied by corrective actions the person willingly takes in their life. If they are not willing to take actions in their life from diet to changing relationships to erase the root cause, it is a waste of time to remove the cord.

If it is a negative cord coming from another person its removal will be a major aid in eliminating the problem, provided the person does not allow the cord to be reattached. This can sometimes be a big challenge, especially if the people are living together or see each other every day at work or school. Oftentimes, physical separation becomes necessary to prevent the cord from continually reattaching and rebuilding. This is especially true if the person generating the negative cord wants to maintain its connection and the energy they receive from the other person through it.

These are very real situations and valuable techniques that solve the problem regardless of how alien they may seem to anyone never exposed to similar situations and techniques.

Intention is a powerful tool when it comes to changing auric energy, whether your own or affecting another person's aura. In many cases, negative cords traveling from one person to another can be removed without further training utilizing the power of intention.

The first step is the person asking for the cord to be removed must truly want it removed and want it removed permanently. If they do not begin with their own conviction, any cord removed will quickly return. In some cases, this intention must be additionally manifested by ridding their life of all vestiges of physical items and pictures that remind them of the person that continues to embrace their aura with a negative, energy-sucking cord.

You can remove a cord from yourself simply by grabbing it between your two hands and physically yanking it out of your aura and casting it aside. Do it with a well set intention and enough vehemence that you make an audible exclamation as you pull it out.

You can remove negative cords from others in the same manner. You can also use tools to assist in this that help focus your own auric power. Special wands of wood and/or crystal that taper to a point are very effective for this purpose. When I say "special" I mean special to you. The more affinity you personally have with an item like a wand or quartz crystal, the more effective it will be when you use it. Even a big quartz crystal by itself works very well to focus a concentrated beam of your own auric energy, which combined with your intention and the intention of the person having the cord removed, successfully rids all but the most stubborn and powerful cords.

When using a wand of a quartz crystal, you should hold it with two hands near to your body with the point aiming upward. Close your eyes and focus your intent to blast the negative cord on the other person into smithereens. Now draw your own aura in tightly to your body by visualization and the physical feel of your aura. Swirl it very fast. Now as you open your eyes and see the cord, rapidly extend your arms, pointing the wand straight at the point it enters the other person's auric field. At the same moment, will your auric energy down your arms, blasting with great power out of the wand or crystal. You can aid the flow of your auric power through your arms and the wand or crystal by audibly making a loud expel of breath as you send out the auric stream. Presto! Negative cord is gone.

Chapter 16

USING THE AURA TO DO AN IN-DEPTH HEALTH BODY SCAN

The human aura, both felt and seen, can be an amazing tool for diagnosing physical, emotional and mental illness in a person. However, it would be a mistake for anyone, particularly a lay person not trained in the medical arts and human body anatomy and physiology, to draw firm conclusions relying solely on what the aura is telling them about someone's health. Collaborating indicators, including physical symptoms and tests, as well as the examination and opinion of a medical professional should also be sought before any advice is given or treatment suggested for any significant health problem.

I am going to provide conclusions I have drawn from over 50 years of observing and studying auras along with a robust but still limited education about the human body and functions. Please use my assessment as only one tool of the diagnosis of the health of any individual. Final determinations should only be made after multiple diagnostic techniques, including those of a medical professional have been applied and considered.

For some years I had a steady stream of people coming to me to have me look at their aura, tell them what I saw and offer an interpretation. Many people had concerns about their health and what steps they could take to improve any existing problems in their body. The aura is a unique health diagnostic tool, as any kind of physical, mental or emotional problem will be glaringly obvious in a person's auric field. You will be able to see the problems easily. But understanding what the specific problems are that correlate to the disruptions you see in the aura is the real challenge.

During decades of observation and study, I came to understand a great deal about what the aura was telling me about a person's state of health. Typically, I would see an aberration in the auric field. An example would be sky blue tendrils emanating from several spots along the aura perimeter. In that instance, tuning into my psychic perception, I would immediately get a "psychic knowing" that I was looking at a potassium deficiency. From a scientific perspective I might as well have picked a name out of a hat. But I learned to trust my psychic intuition even if it had no basis in scientific method or medical knowledge stored in my head.

Despite that trust, I never wanted to give anyone wrong or harmful advice. So just as I recommend to you, I studied human anatomy and physiology, plus read numerous books, ever seeking to learn more about the physical signs and symptoms the human body gives to tell of illness hidden inside.

After looking at someone's aura I would scrutinize many physical aspects that could be collaborating indicators of poor health. These included: the pallor of their skin, the yellow or bloodshot in the whites of their eyes, the dryness and state of their hair, the dilation of their pupils, the state and health telltales of their fingernails, their posture, their gait when they walked, and the smell of their breath when they spoke to me face-to-face, as well as the appearance of their tongue.

I always gave everyone a hug when we met, but I also liked to shake their hand. In addition to energetically being a quick gauge of the strength of their auric field, the dryness or clamminess and warmth or cold of their handshake, as well as the physical firmness of the muscles and the appearance of the skin, spoke insightfully about internal health conditions. Many of these physical indicators, which I had learned either through reading, or through years of observation and correlation to auric symptoms, confirmed my "psychic knowing" as to what the aberration in their aura meant from a health perspective.

With that understanding of how I came to assign meanings to physical, mental and emotional illnesses and disruptions as shown by the aura, here are the things I look at and the step-by-step procedures I use to do a Body Scan for someone.

1. Soul Name: I like to begin by knowing someone's Soul Name. This is the name each person gave themselves before they were ever born into their current body, to help them on their journey. However, they are often unaware of it when I first meet or speak with them. Who am I? Why am I here? Where should I be going or focusing in my life? These are questions answered in your Soul Name. Each Soul Name is unique and the sounds have a powerful resonant effect on the person who bears the name, calling them and motivating them to fulfill their greater purpose in life. If you would like to learn more about Soul Names please visit my Soul Name website, *www.mysoulname.com*. It is far easier for me to psychically tune into someone I have never met if I know their Soul Name first.

2. Aura Strength: (scale of 1-10). This is the very first health indicator I look at when doing a Body Scan. Regardless of all other indicators of problems in the aura, strength of aura as seen by the vividness of the auric field, is a huge indicator of wellness or problems. The auric strength does not tell you what the problems are, or whether they are physical, emotional or mental. You'll need to look at other aspects of the aura to make that determination. But it gives you an excellent base to understand the current vitality of the person.

3. Aura Scintillation: (scale of 1-10). There is a metallic, mirage-like quality to all human auras. It is only seen in Layer 6. Regardless of the primary colors that may be showing in Layer 6, there will be an overall, faint, mirage-like shimmer of metallic colors dancing on the outer edge of the auric field, that is impossible to put in a picture because of its tenuousness and the metallic nature of the colors. You'll just have to see it.

There are five possible colors and most often all five will be present in one degree or another. These metallic shimmers are: Gold, Silver, Copper, Bronze and Electric Blue. As this is the aura layer involved in both the person's integral character and their astral travel abilities, I have always associated these metallic shimmers with both aspects.

If there is a preponderance of bronze it indicates a person that has never consciously traveled with their auric essence and is not very evolved consciously.

A copper preponderance shows someone still quite grounded on Earth, but a little more evolved than the bronze. They probably have not yet done any astral traveling.

A strong showing of silver indicates an individual that certainly astral travels while they are sleeping, but is probably only vaguely aware of it in their conscious thoughts. They are more evolved consciously than the average person, but are probably in the early stages of expanding themselves beyond the "normal" box they were placed in by family and society.

A lot of gold showing in the Layer 6 shimmer, indicates a person that is purposefully exploring and expanding their consciousness. They are an active astral traveler while they are asleep and likely have a good memory of some of their night travels as seen through their dreams.

A preponderance of electric blue in the 6th layer shimmer, shows a person of high consciousness that is also very aware that they are far more than a physical body. They astral travel often, almost every night and often with Lucid Dreaming. They probably have made attempts or had success astral traveling from an awake state as well.

4. Gold Band of Soul Level Happiness: (scale of 1-10). The gold band is seen in the outer edge of Layer 4 regardless of any other colors that may be present in that layer. It is very thin,

Gold Band of Happiness, on a scale of 1-10, picture above showing about a 6

only seen around the head and abdomen, and usually only ½ – 1 inch in thickness, and width is not one of the signs I use to gauge it's strength. It can be barely perceptible or intensely visible and this is the indicator I use to assign it a power level between 1-10, with 10 being highest. After looking at the auras of thousands of people over the last 50 years I can say with certainty that the gold band correlates directly to a person's deep level of happiness with their life. Though superficial happiness can change dramatically with events, both good and bad, from day to day or even within the same day, the gold band intensity does not change easily or quickly, indicating it is emanating from a soul level depth.

5. Endocrine Weakness: This is one of the easier health related conditions to accurately diagnose. You should be three dimensionally aware of the specific location in the body of all the

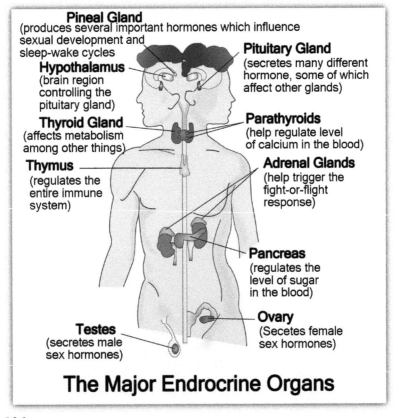

Pineal Gland
(produces several important hormones which influence sexual development and sleep-wake cycles

Hypothalamus
(brain region controlling the pituitary gland)

Pituitary Gland
(secretes many different hormone, some of which affect other glands)

Thyroid Gland
(affects metabolism among other things)

Parathyroids
(help regulate level of calcium in the blood)

Thymus
(regulates the entire immune system)

Adrenal Glands
(help trigger the fight-or-flight response)

Pancreas
(regulates the level of sugar in the blood)

Testes
(secretes male sex hormones)

Ovary
(Secetes female sex hormones)

The Major Endrocrine Organs

endocrine glands, which includes the pineal, pituitary, thalamus, hypothalamus, thyroid, parathyroid, thymus, adrenals, pancreas, ovaries and testes. When you are looking at Layer 5, three dimensionally observe the location of each of the endocrine glands. If there is no problem, you will not even be able to distinguish any difference in the appearance of that area from any other area in Layer 5. If there is a problem with the function of that gland, the area of the gland will appear darker in black or gray colors. The darker it is the bigger the problem. Some of these glands are quite small, like the size of a nut, so you have to know exactly where to look and look closely to distinguish them.

6. Auric Parasites: Think of these as the "Blobs." They are opaque dark areas seen on the outer part of Layer 6. People have differing beliefs as to what they are, but one thing I can state with certainty is they are energy drains on a person's mental, physical and emotional vitality and should be removed.

Auric parasites are seen as a cloudy, translucent, black color, usually between the size of a fist and the hand with fingers splayed out. But they can be half the size of a fist or twice the size of a spread out hand on occasion. The larger they are the more tenaciously they cling to a person's aura. You can distinguish them from other similar looking black shapes that indicate problems in the person, because blobs make continuous sinuous movements as if they were alive. Similar black shapes appearing in the aura and showing other problems are static, they don't move as if they are alive.

When you are looking for auric parasites you need to have the person you are looking at slowly turn completely around 360 degrees so you can see every side of their aura. The blobs will only show up at one location on the auric field and cannot be seen through the body if they are on the other side.

To most easily remove a blob on someone you need to blast them with your auric energy focused through a large, center-pointed quartz crystal held firmly in both hands, with the point facing away from your hands. Begin by holding the crystal in both hands, next to your chest, with the point pointing upward. With your eyes closed, coalesce your own energy by pulling your auric field in close to your body. Will it to be so and open your senses to feel your aura concentrating nearer and nearer to your body. Once your aura is densely coalesced, begin to spin it rapidly and omni-directionally. When you are ready, open your eyes and look at the location of the blob. Take a big breath of air and quickly thrust your hands holding the crystal forward, pointing it directly at the blob standing at a distance about 3 feet away. Exhale forcibly and push the concentrated energy of your aura out of your core, down your arms, shooting out of the crystal and blast the blob. Most of the time the blob will instantly disappear. If it doesn't and it is still there, do the same procedure once again.

The blobs seem to absorb all the energy of your auric blast and there are no detrimental effects to the person they were on from your concentrated energy blast at them. Quite the contrary, they will almost always feel like a great weight has been lifted off of them and they will experience a marked increase in their energy level and happiness.

Some people will have no energy parasites, but about half the people will average one to four. I have seen as many as twenty on some people. Each blob needs to be blasted individually. Energy parasites seem to accumulate most on people who frequent darker places such as bars and nightclubs and people who are taking actions in their lives that are not the most noble or expanding of their light. Because most of us go through both good days and bad during the course of months, there is ample opening for blobs to attach. Because of this it is helpful to look for and remove them at least once every six months.

7. Negative Cords: These are cords of energy that run from one person to another. They pierce all layers of the aura and can travel vast distances. However, greater distances do weaken the strength of the cord. There are many good cords of energy as well, and they show up with harmonious energy flow through the cord as indicated by color and reciprocal flow. Negative cords show up with a highly agitated, disruptive flow through the conduit of the cord. There is no doubt you are looking at negative energy, harmful to some aspect of the person when your see it. I explain more about cords in Chapters 14 and 15.

A Body Scan merely alerts someone to cords they are either sending out to other people (master cords) or cords that others are sending out and attaching to them (slave cords), or cords that are reciprocally created and mutually beneficial, (reciprocal cords). The body scan by itself can do no more than identify how many cords of each type there are. If someone wants the cords removed, that would be beyond the scope of a Body Scan. Chapter 15 explains the procedures for removing negative energy cords. You would first need to determine the origin and destination of each cord and what created it. You could do a quick cord severing similar to the procedure to remove Auric Parasites, but if you haven't determined the root cause from a deeper   exploration and eliminated the cause, the cord will quickly return and reattach.

8. Vitamin and Mineral Deficiencies: No matter how good our diet might be, almost everyone is deficient in one or more vitamins and minerals necessary for optimum health. Many people take daily vitamins and mineral supplements in the form of pills or liquid concentrates. But they do so blindly, not really knowing if they are wasting money taking something they don't need, or not taking something their body actually lacks and needs. When you are looking at Layer 5 of the aura you will always see tiny undulating threads or ribbons of various colors radiating out from the body and through the 5th layer. Sometimes they will be located only on a certain area of the aura. In that case, you are being pointed to the specific area of a problem. More often, they show up randomly throughout the fifth layer. These threads and ribbons of color indicate vitamin and mineral deficiencies in the body. The wider the thread or ribbon the greater the deficiency. Following are the colors I have been able to associate with various nutritional deficiencies as I have observed auras and the corresponding health of people over the last decades:

Sky Blue = Potassium	Turqupose = Riboflavin
Lime Green = Vitamin C	Purple = Maganese
Light Violet = Biotin	Oxblood Red = Vitamin K
Bright Red = Pyrodoxine	Dark Orange = Iodine
Carrot Orange = Vitamin A	Beige = Magnesium
Alabaster = Niacin	Pale Amber = Vitamin E
Silver Gray = Vitamin D	Straw Yellow = Thiamin
Rose Pink = Selenium	Cobalt Blue = Cobalamin
Rust Brown = Iron	Pale Green = Copper
Lemon Yellow = Zinc	Pale Red = Pantothenic Acid
Emerald Green = Chromium	Pure White = Calcium

9. Protein Deficiency: This can be a challenge for vegetarians, particularly if they are vegans and eat no animal proteins. Though they may eat plenty of vegetable sources of protein they often are not getting a healthy balance of the various amino acids that make up the complete protein needs of the human body. All the essential amino acids are found in animal protein, but they are not all found in single source vegetable protein. Vegetarians must eat a good mix of non-animal foods to get the complete balance of essential amino acids all people need. Protein deficiency is also observed in Layer 5 of the aura. You look along the inner edge closest to the body to see this indicator. If the person is receiving adequate complete protein you will notice nothing unusual about this inner area of Layer 5. But if they are lacking in complete protein or simply deficient in their protein intake, the inner layer of Layer 5 will have a dirty white opacity to it. The bigger this band of dirt is the more severe the protein deficiency.

10. Internal Parasites: In other words, creepy crawly bugs living inside of you and eating you! And you thought humans were the top of the food chain.

There are four common types of harmful bugs that can be in your body or your pets. Helminthes are multi-celled worms such as tapeworms which are very flat and often several feet long. Pinworms and roundworms are their close cousins. Flukes are another cousin, basically smaller worms that are flat and wide instead of narrow and round. Flukes are particularly dangerous as they tend to like to inhabit and live off of your body organs rather than in the intestinal tract. They can do more damage in an organ and are more difficult to kill and remove from sensitive organs. Adult worms can hatch from eggs in your body but the adults cannot multiply.

Protozoa, another body invader, are single cell critters such as Giardia or Cryptosporidium. Unlike the worms, Protozoa love to reproduce and multiply inside both humans and animals inside the   intestinal tract. The ability to multiply inside the human body can cause serious infections. All the parasitic critters are usually acquired by coming in contact with contaminated feces of either humans or animals.

Though parasites love to find homes in your intestinal tract, nearly every organ and part of your body is subject to parasite invasion and occupation. Here's a great link giving a long list of the types of parasites you can acquire, how you get them and the damage they can do.

People with cats or dogs are much more likely to become infected by these nasty bugs as the adults or the eggs are often found in soil that has come in contact with infected animal feces. Dogs notoriously like to smell, step on, and even roll around in other dogs feces. Both dogs and cats like to defecate at spots where other dogs and cats have done their business so they get infected often. Cats even try extra hard to infect themselves by using their paws to stir up the contaminated dirt to cover their own feces. Then the animals come into the house and drop the worms and protozoa all over the house from the soil still clinging to their feet. The human inhabitants then walk barefoot or in their socks around the house and they acquire the bugs.

Parasites are more likely to be acquired in homes, schools and workplaces with poor sanitation of the food and water supplies, or while on international trips or in areas or homes known to have a problem with parasites.

Parasites are tough and can live for several years in the human intestinal tract without obvious symptoms. Doing an auric scan for the bugs is a very helpful way to be aware of a potential problem and initiate a cleanse to eliminate them.

Parasites in the aura are common and easy to spot. Whether they are located in an organ like the liver or brain, or in the intestinal tract they make tiny exploding spots, about the size of a match head, in Layer 1 of the aura over the area they are located.

Chapter 17

DIAGNOSING THE HEALTH OF THE ROOT KI / CHAKRA ENERGY CENTERS

Once you are able to clearly see all of the 7 Root Ki Energy Center Spheres as described in Chapter 6, you can begin looking deeper at the indicators, which can tell an amazing array of insightful details about a persons well-being.

Quartz Crystal Wands

A very useful tool for healing problems in the Root Ki Energy Spheres is a quality quartz crystal. The best should be natural, uncut and unpolished. They should have a center point, be quite clear and mostly free of internal or surface imperfections. If it is double-terminated that is an extra, but unneeded bonus. The crystal should be 6 to 12 inches long and about 1 1/2- 2 1/2 inches in diameter, with the smaller diameter applying to the smaller crystals. The closer you can get to those specifications the easier you will be able to use your quartz crystal as a valuable healing tool.

Many people have heard of the piezoelectric effect in quartz crystals and assume this has something to do with their usefulness as healing tools. To activate the piezoelectric effect actually requires mechanical stress in the form of pressure or stretching to be applied to the crystal, and this does not occur while you are simply holding it in your hand. Nevertheless, I have found clear, wand-shaped, center-pointed quartz crystals to be wonderful tools to focus the auric energy coming from the healer and directed at the patient. The power is in you, not the crystal. But the crystal is an excellent, natural wand to funnel, amplify and focus, the auric power you send through it. If instead of using a crystal, you pointed your finger, though it too comes to a tip, in most cases it is a far less effective way than a quality quartz crystal to focus a narrow beam of highly charged auric energy.

To use a quartz crystal to optimum effect, you need to be able to swirl and concentrate your own auric energy and visualize and coalesce the needed color in your auric field. Do this by holding the quartz crystal in both hands against your chest, with the tip pointing up. Close your eyes and sense in your mind and feel within the cells of your body, the movement of your inner auric field. Silently command, mentally visualize and internally reach out and feel your aura moving inside of you. Call it and pull it in very close and dense to your body. Swirl it faster and faster. Transform it into the color you need to help someone with their auric problems. When you are ready, take a deep breath, then with a forceful exhale thrust the crystal out pointing toward the energy sphere you are working on and follow the additional procedures outlined below as appropriate.

Following are explanations of all the energy aberrations and indicators you can see in the 7 Root Ki Energy Center Spheres, the abbreviations to use when recording a person's energy condition during a Body Scan, and the things you can do to affect beneficial change when the person is having challenges:

CM = Clockwise Movement: A clockwise movement is encountered about 10% of the time in the northern hemisphere. I've yet to visit the southern hemisphere so I don't know if that correlates to the other half of the planet. When you encounter an energy center spinning almost exclusively clockwise, it shows the person has an exceptionally strong focus in that area. For instance, someone that was a fitness fanatic would likely have a clockwise spinning Wz energy center.

CCM = Counter Clockwise Movement: This is encountered with about 1 out of 4 people in the northern hemisphere for at least one of their energy centers, and often more than one. It is the opposite of the fanatic energy of the clockwise motion. A counterclockwise energy center rotations shows a person who has a totally care less attitude about that energy center aspect of their life. For instance, a couch potato who looked at walking to the fridge to get more food as exercise, would surely have a counterclockwise spinning Wz.

DS = Debilitated State: An energy center that is limping along, with three or more of the other problems outlined here, should be considered to be in a debilitated state. This person has been having problems with this energy center either for a very long time or recently in very intense ways. Either way, an energy center in a debilitated state will take extra time and effort to fix, both on the part of the healer and the healee.

EM = Erratic Movement: About 5% of the time you'll encounter an energy center that cannot seem to make up its mind about anything. It will spin clockwise for a few seconds, then be omnidirectional for some seconds, then go back to clockwise or maybe to counterclockwise. Its opacity may vary just in the minute you are looking at it. It may puff up larger and shrink down smaller and push out in one direction so it no longer has a spherical shape, all in less than a minute or two. This indicates a very confused person about that aspect of their body or life. For instance, a person with moral values to be a virgin until marriage, who is sorely tempted to break that conviction by their lust for their current partner, would likely have erratic movement in their Vm.

ET = Energy Tumor: This is usually a problem that sounds worst than it is and is common in around 80% of auras I have looked closely at in my life. Energy tumors are seen as black blob-like spots of varying sizes on the Root Ki whirling sphere of energy. The tumor usually spins in unison with the energy ball as it is whirling around. If it does, it shows an old problem that the person has probably already dealt with. The original problem caused a tear in the energy center sphere that has never been healed. Though the original challenge may have vanished, the remaining tumor continues to create a weakness in the energy sphere at that point, making it more likely that a similar problem will return.

If the black spot of the tumor does not revolve around in unison with the spinning energy field, but hovers in place on the outside surface of the sphere while the sphere spins below, it indicates a problem that is still vexing the person today.

The former can easily be healed simply by focusing a wide beam of energy through a quartz crystal washing over the entire energy center sphere. Do this by mentally picturing the light beam as you physically feel the swirl of energy inside you channeled through your arms and out the crystal. Be sure to begin with the firm intent to heal that specific tumor. The latter instance requires more in-depth healing, beginning with understanding the root cause of the problem.

EV = Energy Vortex: Vortexes are small whirlpools of energy seen on the outside surface of a Root Ki Energy Sphere. They are also fairly common, occurring at least 50% of the time on at least one energy center. Looking just like a mini tornado, their wide top tapers down into a narrow tip as it drops deeper into the center of the energy field. They hold approximate position in the energy sphere and move and rotate in unison with the movement and rotation of the sphere with a just little wavering of position. You can readily see the vortexes as there will be a noticeable dimple in the surface of the energy sphere at the top of the vortex. The vortexes are always spinning either constantly clockwise or constantly counterclockwise.

Energy Vortexes on a Root Ki Sphere are disruptive to a

smooth omnidirectional movement. Their errant energy should be harmoniously countered through visualization and coalescing and sending your auric energy through a quartz crystal wand pointed closely at the Root Ki Sphere. Spin the wand in a small circle about 1-2 inches in diameter, in the opposite direction of the energy vortex movement. Usually, 10-15 seconds will suffice to eliminate the vortex.

MECT = Master Energy Cord To: If you are sending a dominating energy to another person, whether they are near or far from your proximity, it shows as a cord leaving one of your energy centers and traveling to a point, often unseen, beyond your auric field. It is distinguished as a Master Cord because you can visibly see the energy flow inside the cord and it is flowing only one direction, which is away from you and toward the other person. The outward flow distinguishes it as a Master Cord, meaning you are sending a dominating and overbearing energy to another person. This may not be something you are consciously doing. But if such a cord becomes apparent in your auric field you should determine who it is going to and seriously apprise your relationship. Also, be on the lookout for additional cords as you can have more than one, emanating from multiple energy centers.

In most instances, it is healthier for both people connected to the cord to sever the cord as outlined in Chapter 15, using energy focused through a quartz crystal and a sharp severing motion cutting the cord. Then heal the place where it came through the auric field with golden light through the quartz crystal.

OM = Omnidirectional Movement: The healthiest movement of Root Ki Energy Sphere is omnidirectional. This is regardless of any other factors such as speed, size or opacity. The other factors are certainly important as well, but they a secondary compared to the omnidirectional spin. You can easily distinguish an omnidirectional spin from a detrimental Erratic Movement. Where the Erratic Movement will be chaotic with fits and starts, the omnidirectional movement will flow smoothly, effortlessly and harmoniously changing directions. It all occurs so smoothly you almost need to remind yourself that you are seeing the sphere spin in many different directions. The transition from one direction to another is seamless.

Omnidirectional Movement is observed about 50% of the time with any given Root Ki Energy Sphere. If you do not see an omnidirectional spin that is a red flag to immediately look deeper and try to determine why it is missing. Is there a negative cord coming in or going out from that energy center that is altering its natural movement? Is there a rip, tear or tumor located in that area of the auric field affecting the normal movement of the energy sphere? Is there a cord coming from another energy center that is negatively affecting this one? For instance perhaps the Wz energy center is spinning erratically. Yet it has no rips, tears or tumors that would indicate it is energetically unhealthy. Looking closer you may see a cord connecting from the heart and another from the mind and both of these centers show serious problems. Perhaps the person just broke up with their girlfriend or boyfriend. Their heart center is aching and their mind center is in a turmoil. Both of these energy centers may be sending cording into the Wz center and causing physical distress.

REC = Reciprocal Energy Cord: Where both Slave and Master Energy Cords are detrimental in most instances, the reciprocal cord, showing an energy flow both in and out, indicates a very healthy, supportive and expansive relationship. Everyone should have Reciprocal Energy Cords connecting from every energy center to one or more people beyond the auric field. Parents, children, friends, lovers: all are hopefully worthy of Reciprocal Energy Cords connecting to at least one of your Energy Spheres. Like a breath of pure fresh air, these cords invigorate and expand any Energy Sphere they connect to. You can tell a lot about a person by seeing how many or how few reciprocal cords are transiting their auric field.

SECF = Slave Energy Cord From: If someone near or far from you by physical distance is connecting to you with a cord that is controlling you in any way, physically, mentally or emotionally, it will show as a Slave Cord connection, as in they are the master and you are the slave. Or more correctly, they are the dominating energy and you are the submissive. These are not healthy cords and stifle the normal energy movement, size and opacity of any energy center to which they are attached. The person sending the cord to you is probably completely unaware that they are doing so. Nevertheless the cord is retarding your own energy and should be severed as is covered in Chapter 15. You can have more than one Slave Cord coming in to connect to multiple energy spheres. You can also have Slave Cords coming in from more than one person who is consciously or unconsciously sending energy to dominate you. Slave cords show a movement of energy flowing in from outside your auric field.

TB = Too Big: Balance is the key word when it comes to your body energy. There is no right or wrong size for the Root Ki Energy Spheres. In a completely healthy aura they will all be within 10% - 15% of the size of one another. If one or more have a greater size difference than 20% it indicates an area of imbalance in the persons life. For instance, if the Vm sphere is 30% larger than any other Root Ki Energy Sphere, while the Ka sphere was 25% smaller, this would indicate a person who obsesses about sex and is disinterested in mental challenges. A person with a larger heart sphere and a smaller Ka, would show a person ruled by their heart when they make choices and decisions. Someone with a large Wz, a large Ka and a smaller Ja, would indicate a person concerned with a high level of fitness with both their mind and their body, but more of a disconnect from their heart.

TF = Too Fast: Speed is also an indicator of balance. Take note of which Energy Spheres are spinning faster than the others. Are there any signs that would lead you to conclude the faster spin is something to be concerned about? Or perhaps just the opposite: if no other detrimental signs are showing, it is simply indicative of a very healthy Energy Sphere. The exception would be if it is spinning much faster than any of the other spheres, than it would be like a person that has had too much caffeine in regards to the areas of influence of that Energy Sphere.

TL = Too Little: An Energy sphere that is noticeably smaller than the other six Root Ki Energy Spheres is usually a problem. If so, you will see other supporting indicators such as rips, tears, tumors or negative cords. Using focused energy through a quartz crystal, with green light, while pointing the crystal toward the Energy Sphere, you can make spinning motions that push outward and expand the sphere. This will be a temporary fix, but the person should notice the difference in the way they feel and hopefully be open to additional recommendations they can pursue on their own to continue improvement.

TS = Too Slow: Like too fast, too slow is also not a good sign if it is noticeably slower than the other Energy Spheres. People who are suffering from depression, anxiety and Bipolar often show one or more Energy spheres with a lethargic speed. If there is a problem, there will always be additional indicators on that energy sphere such as rips, tears, tumors or negative cords. If no other additional indicators of a problem are present than it may simply be an energetic area the person pays scant attention to in their life and so far has not suffered detrimental consequences from being out of balance. If you want to give a temporary jolt to the energy center to speed it up, use red focused light through a quartz crystal with a vigorous clockwise spinning motion while holding the crystal and pointing in the direction of the Energy Sphere.

W = Wall: Though walls can be found surrounding any of the seven Energy Spheres they are most often seen around the Heart Sphere of the Ja and were built by the person themselves, following one or more traumas. When someone is hurt in any way they begin to build energy walls to protect themselves from similar pain in the future. If someone has been hurt in love, as is often encountered, they will have a wall around their heart. If someone has been physically traumatized they may have a wall around their Wz. Someone that has suffered an ordeal like rape, will often have a wall around their heart, another around the physical center of their Wz, and still another around their mental center of the Ka. A soldier traumatized in war, may have walls around the same three energy centers plus around the Za, which is the root of primal fears.

Though walls at the time of injury are very helpful self-defense mechanisms, they seldom fall down as time passes on, even though their usefulness probably passed long ago. In fact, over time after the trauma fades but the wall still remains, it becomes a serious impediment to healthy energy and successful, mutually beneficial and reciprocal relations with other people.

Walls are clearly seen when looking at the Energy Spheres. They will be a non-moving opaque white sphere covering the inner Energy Sphere which you will be able to see swirling inside. The thickness of the wall is determined by how opaque it is and subsequently how easily you can see the Energy Sphere it encapsulates.

When you see a wall it is best to talk to the person about it. When you mention it, most people will immediately be aware and acknowledge they have a wall on that energy center. More importantly they will almost always know why. To best help them you need to gently probe to find out if the wall is still needed today or if it is holding them back from fulfilling relationships and personal expansion and progression. This is often the case.

If the person is willing to have the wall come down, or even be partially diminished, you can help them. If they are unwilling or unsure, you need to wait until they are ready and willing. Otherwise, any good you effect would quickly be undone and the walls rebuilt by the person who was still clinging to them.

If they are willing and supportive of diminishing or removing their walls, have them stand about four feet away from the tip of the outstretched quartz crystal. Follow the procedure outlined at the beginning of this chapter to pull in and swirl your aura. Imbue your aura with a rainbow light. When you are ready, ask the person to begin slowly turning around and around standing in place. As they do so, thrust the crystal forward pointing it at the level of the wall. As they spin around and around lovingly flow rainbow light down your arms and out the crystal, bathing the area on their body where the wall resides. You will be able to see the wall diminish. If the person doesn't want the wall eliminated, but only diminished a certain percentage, have them continue spinning around until the opacity clears up to that point. If they want the wall completely removed, have them continue spinning around until the wall has vanished and the Energy Sphere is showing brightly.

Chapter 18

INTERESTING EXPERIENCES WITH AURAS

Poker

Throughout my life, in addition to actual experiences, I have considered various endeavors that would allow me to benefit from my strong ability to see and feel auras. Yet it is astounding how many ventures you would think at first thought would be perfect fits for an aura reader, are found not to be so upon closer scrutiny.

For example, in my youth, I envisioned myself as the most successful poker player the world had ever known, as anyone bluffing would have their facade revealed in a sick-looking green color that appears right around a person's head when they are lying or hiding the truth. My Dad was a master poker player. He served in the submarine services and would be away on mission deployment for months at a time every year. My mother missed him when he was gone, but enjoyed the extra money he sent back home every month from his poker winnings from captive, inexperienced players, locked inside the submarine as it cruised beneath the ocean.

On more than one occasion when my father was home, I would ask him teach me his poker skills. And on the rare occasions he played poker at home I always sat on the periphery as an observer, fascinated to look at the players auras as they tried to not give away any indications of the cards they held in their hand. I hoped that with knowledge of my father's skills combined with my ability to to discern when people were being less than forthcoming with the truth, I would be virtually unstoppable in a poker game once I became an adult. Reality did not work out that way.

I soon learned that good poker players are experts at masking their feelings and completely eliminating unwanted facial expressions or hand, face or body movements. And though I'm sure none of the men that played with my father even knew what an aura was, many of them had expressionless auras as well while they were paying poker! No vomit green aura around their head when they were bluffing; no increase or decrease in their auric strength indicating anything different; and no increased activity in their brain auric activity or heart energy center movement, color or anything. It was like they were zombies! The amateurs showed plenty of auric signs. But the guys that were good- their auras were as expressionless as their faces.

My father actually memorized every card that was shown face up during a poker hand, to mentally calculate which cards were left in the deck. He was had amazing accuracy correctly knowing the majority of cards other players were holding. This was a game skill I was never able to master or become even halfway proficient.

He also looked for 'tells' in opposing players: slight motions of the body such as touching their earlobe, blinking their eyes rapidly, taking a deep breath or other virtually unnoticeable actions that signaled the strength of the hand they were holding and rather they were bluffing or had the cards to back their play when they didn't fold, but stayed in the game. But really good players like my father had learned to suppress or eliminate their 'tells' long ago. Any 'tells' they showed were more likely preplanned false 'tells' to set their opponents up for a big fall down the road.

For instance, to set up a false tell, my Dad would touch his left earlobe very quickly and slightly whenever he was bluffing.

He would purposefully lose two to three hands with small pots while showing that tell and then be found to be bluffing, when he showed his cards at the end of the hand. When the pot grew large and he had what he had what he had ascertained to be the best hand at the table, he would give his false tell. Even experienced players, having observed his previous false 'tells' would think he was bluffing. They would insist on piling on the raises forcing my Dad and anyone that wanted to stay in the game to match them. The pots quickly grew very large and there would be a lot of shocked players at the end when my father would lay down the winning hand and rake in all the chips.

Even my aspirations for succeeding at poker with amateur players came to naught. Though unlike the good players, their auric activity did give away their true intentions, and though I did learn many skills from my father that should have helped me win, I had one irreparable personal flaw: I could not bluff! If I tried to tell a lie my face got flush, every time. It may have remained stoically impassive, but it still got redder. It was something I had no control of and effectively made me one of the worst poker players on the planet!

Medical Diagnosis and Auric Healing

Another field I considered would be an appropriate one for my abilities as an aura reader was in medical diagnosis and as an energy healer using the aura. This idea came to me later in life after I had become very proficient in understanding what the many aspects of an aura meant, from the colors, to the squiggles, to the speed and size of the energy centers. I could clearly see specific areas in the body where things were not right and often could trace cords that would show the source of the illness or condition, which sometimes was within the person and other times came from an outside source.

Being able to feel the aura as well as see it was immensely helpful in understanding the severity of a problem. A chronic condition was actually physically hot! And a serious one would always be noticeably warmer than any other location on the auric field.

I invested many days over several years in observing the auras of sick people and correlating what I saw and felt to the illness or disease they had contracted. I also bought many books and studied them to have a better understanding of the human body: how it functioned, how everything interconnected and what physical symptoms might indicate.

It wasn't until I felt I was fully ready to help people truly understand the root cause of their maladies and banish their illness for good that I came up against the brick wall of orthodoxy. Apparently, according to the law, I would be "practicing medicine without a license" and be subject to fines and even possible imprisonment! Even if I helped someone the health that medical orthodoxy had given up on and proclaimed as "incurable", I would still be punished, because I hadn't participated in the orthodox schooling and didn't have a nice piece of paper on my wall attesting to my graduation from a certified school of medicine. So another possible aura career bit the dust.

Daughter's experience

There is an upside to this story however. Though I couldn't openly help people I didn't know, I could use my knowledge and abilities to help my family members, which I have freely done over many years. My youngest daughter, who is now 17, is a prime example of the benefits: she has never gone to a doctor in her entire life.

The one exception was last year when she was in the park with friends and landed badly jumping off a swing. The medics came and she was carefully transported to the emergency room with a broken back. Because of the location and type of injury there wasn't anything they could really do to help her other than ease her pain with drugs, which she tried, but didn't really receive benefit. Thankfully there was no paralysis or loss of feeling in any part of her body.

We brought her home and set her bed up in the living room as their was no way we could get her downstairs to her bedroom or be there quickly if she needed us. For many days she was virtually immobile. But continued treatments with magnets, diet, herbal teas and auric energy worked their magic. Within a few weeks she was up and about and within a couple of months it was as if the accident had never happened.

My experience

I suppose I am the best example of all, as I have successfully diagnosed and treated myself for many decades. I rarely get ill and when I do, auric treatments along with herbal potions quickly bring be back to full vibrancy. I even used the power of the aura along with other alternative treatments to heal myself from a devastating injury in 2014.

My friend Skye and I had taken my 12 foot raft, powered by a 5 hp propane motor, about 1 mile up a very remote, wilderness section of the Klamath River in Northern California. We motored into a landing amidst some boulder near shore and began to explore the area. While I was walking on some small boulders about 50 yards from the raft, I slipped and fell straight down on a rock landing with a bone crunching blast of pain sole on my left knee. The entire weight of my falling body impacted on my kneecap. Immediately, I experienced the most horrifying, excruciating pain I had ever felt or imagined! My knee and thigh were in such agonizing pain and completely unable to move even a millimeter that I was sure I had shattered my kneecap and snapped my thighbone.

As I lay in the shallow water, and looked at the obstacle course in front of me strewn with beach ball size boulders, the raft, my only way back to civilization and help, seemed very far away. Skye was unable to lift me or drag me. With no other recourse and terrifying pain at every movement, I drug myself on my elbows, which soon became bloodied and painfully tender, until I eventually reached the raft. Then to my dismay there was absolutely no way to pull myself over the pontoon and up into the raft even with Skyes help. My leg could not bend at all and I could not pull myself up over the rounded pontoon from my prone position.

I poignantly realized this was a real moment of truth; a time where all I had learned and experienced about auric power was either going to help me now or fail me and leave me to an unkind fate. Laying half submerged in the water, I momentarily ignored my pain and called in my aura, coalescing it tightly inside my body so there was no auric field extending beyond my skin. Then I began to spin my aura, faster and faster until it was a whirling tornado of blinding light inside of me. I turned my palms upward and called in all the energy of the earth, air and water that surrounded me to augment and further empower my own auric field.

Normally, very little outside energy would come in simply by calling it. But the action of bringing my own auric field in very close and spinning it exceptionally rapidly created a venturi affect, a auric pressure vacuum that sucked in far more energy from outside the body than would normally be possible and augmented my own auric field.

I could feel the mighty upwelling of energy inside of me. I sent it down my arms and into my hands and with a hand on either side of my leg bathed my inured knees and thigh in brilliant white light. The pain quickly lessened and the white light momentarily empowered me, enough so that with Skye's help I was able to stand and even walk gingerly with a straight, stiff leg over to the raft and plop down inside of it.

There were many other obstacles on the trip back to civilization but they were all negotiated, albeit with much pain which was still almost unbearably intense. About 3 hours later we arrived at the emergency room and after x-rays I got the bad news: my kneecap had shattered and my tendons joining my thigh muscles to my leg bones had shredded and ripped off the bone. I was referred to an orthopedic surgeon whom I saw the next day. The good news is my thigh bone was intact and had not fractured.

The orthopedic surgeon took some additional detailed x-rays, which just confirmed the original diagnosis of the emergency room. He asked me to get an MRI the next day so he would have a clear map to repair the damage and said I needed to schedule surgery within the next 5 days.

It was actually 3 days before I was able to get the MRI and get back to the orthopedic surgeons for a final consultation before surgery. During those preceding days, I did intense auric energy work on my knee. Skye and my wife Sumara also gave me multiple treatments using bioenergy. I spent most of my time on my back in bed with my leg iced and elevated. Though I am a vegetarian, I also added beef gelatin as a supplement and took lots of turmeric to aid in pain and restoration. I also encompassed my knee with many small, powerful magnets taped on with the south pole facing my knee.

Traditional magnetic therapy says to use the north pole for all treatments. But when I was in college I did experiments with the energy from the south and north poles and found the south pole energy sped up metabolic and biologic action while the north pole slowed it down. I wanted my healing to speed up, not slow down, so I used the south pole face of the magnets against my skin.

After taking a quick look at my greatly swollen knee area, the doctor left me in the patient room and went out to review the MRI scans. He returned a few minutes later with a very strange look on his face. "I can't explain what I am seeing." he said.

"If I didn't know better, I would not think that the knee from our x-rays was even the same knee that the MRI scanned. However, there is a matching piece of bone that came up with the ripped tendon on the quadriceps muscle, that shows up in both the x-rays and the MRI, so I know these are both pictures of your knee, just 3 days apart. But what they are showing seems hardly possible."

Then came the really good news! "You are not going to need

surgery after all." He said with surprise in his voice.

"Somehow the ligaments that had torn away from your bones have reattached and seem to actually have already regenerated some in this short time. I want you to come back next week so we can see if this continues. But at this point there is nothing surgery can do that your body is not already doing for you." He explained somewhat baffled.

My healing continued rapidly after that and I never returned to the see the doctor again. A little over a week later I was walking and doing most of my normal chores and within a couple of months of the initial injury I was 100% back as if the injury had never occurred! That's the power of the aura, aided by ice (temperature energy), herbs (chemical energy) and magnets (magnetic energy).

CONCLUSION

To read more from a spiritual perspective about auras and the powers and abilities that come with them, please read Chapter 81 "*The Power of the Aura*" in the **Oracles of Celestine Light**, which is available to read for free online, www.celestinelight.org. Another short section in Chapter 97 of the **Oracles of Celestine Light** also speaks about auras and is worth quoting here.

165 "This is why it is so important for you to become sensitive to what you feel with your aura because with this you can sense far more energies than your eyes can see, or your ears can hear, or your nose can smell, or your mouth can taste, or your skin can feel.

166 In time, with experience, you will be able to identify nearly everything, both from your world and others, merely by how it's aura feels as it comes in contact with yours.

167 Truly, your aura is the sum of your being. It embodies every iota of your body and every iota of your spirit. It is connected to all existence from the most inconsequential bug to the essence of the Celestine Light of Elohim.

168 A worthy pursuit of all Children of Light is to know yourself so fully that your aura is your best friend, for in this you will be in harmony with all creation. Then to strive to be so perfected in your body, mind and spirit that you can be in resonance with all things as you desire, even as are the Elohim.

169 In this life, you will never achieve that level of perfection, but by striving for it, with focus and faith, but without fanaticism, you will still gain more than you can imagine and amazing will be the wonders that shall be yours. You will truly be in the world but not of it."

Becoming sensitive, aware and understanding of auras will make the whole world a wonderfully different place for you. Enjoy the journey!

Namaste,

Embrosewyn Tazkuvel

ABOUT THE AUTHOR

One of my first childhood memories was of seeing beautiful rainbow auras of light around the heads of people young and old. It began a lifetime of observation, study and experimentation with a wide variety of psychic and paranormal phenomena that has now eclipsed six decades.

Married to my exploration of the supernatural has been a deep spiritual journey to understand and commune with the source of all the magic I found in the world. It has not been merely an intellectual exercise for me. In times more than I can count, I have experienced the wonder and power of the supernatural. Call it magic, magick or miracles, I know they are real, because I have lived and experienced them, time and time again.

I realize my life's journey has been a true blessing greater than I can ever pay back. This has certainly influenced me with a passionate desire to help the people of the world. Many of my books are written with that goal in mind. I believe there is greatness inside every person, calling for someone even greater to emerge. Knowing the secrets to unleashing the magic inside of you is more empowering than anything you can imagine. Your possibilities are as limitless as your imagination, coupled with your knowledge, and your desire to make it so.

I've been fortunate to have traveled to many countries around the world and have interacted with people from the president of the country to the family living in a shack with a dirt floor. Being among people of many cultures, religions and social standings, watching them in their daily lives, seeing their hopes and aspirations for their children and the joys they have with their families and friends, has continually struck me with a deep feeling of oneness. I've been with elderly people as they breathed their last breath and at the birth of babies when they take their first. It's all very humbling. This amazing world we live in and the wonderful people that fill it have given me so much. Writing and sharing the secrets of how everyone can experience magic in their life, is my way to give back as much as I can to as many people as I can.

OTHER CAPTIVATING, THOUGHT-PROVOKING BOOKS BY EMBROSEWYN

CELESTINE LIGHT MAGICKAL SIGILS OF HEAVEN AND EARTH

What would happen if you could call upon the blessings of angels and amplify their miracles with the pure essence of spiritual magick?

Miracles manifest! That is the exciting reality that awaits you in *Celestine Light Magickal Sigils of Heaven and Earth.*

Calling upon the higher realm power of angels, through intentional summoning using specific magickal sigils and incantations, is considered to be the most powerful magick of all. But there is a magickal method even greater. When you combine calling upon a mighty angel with adding synergistic sigils and words of power, the amplification of the magickal energy can be astounding and the results that are manifested truly miraculous. This higher technique of magick is the essence of *Celestine Light Magickal Sigils of Heaven and Earth.*

This is the third book of the Magickal Celestine Light series and is an intermediate level reference book for students and practitioners of Celestine Light Magick. It contains a melding of the sigils and names of 99 of the 144 Angels found in *Angels of Miracles and Manifestation,* coupled with synergistic sigils and magickal incantations found within *Words of Power and Transformation.* To fully be able to implement the potent combination of angel magick and words of power magick revealed in this book, the practitioner should have previously read and have available as references the earlier two books in the series.

When magickal incantations and their sigils are evoked in conjunction with the summoning of an angel for a focused purpose, the magickal results are often exceptional. The potent combination of calling upon angels and amplifying your intent with words of power and sigils of spiritual magick creates an awesome, higher magickal energy that can manifest everyday miracles. Employing this potent form of magick can convert challenges into opportunities, powerfully counter all forms of negative magick, entities, phobias, fears and people, greatly enhance good fortune, and help change ordinary lives into the extraordinary.

ANGELS OF MIRACLES AND MANIFESTATION
144 Names, Sigils and Stewardships To Call the Magickal Angels of Celestine Light

You are not alone. Whatever obstacle or challenge you face, whatever threat or adversary looms before you, whatever ability you seek to gain or mountain of life you want to conquer, divine angelic help is ready to intervene on your behalf. When the unlimited power of magickal angels stand with you, obstacles become opportunities, low times become springboards for better days, relationships blossom, illness becomes wellness, challenges become victories and miracles happen!

In *Angels of Miracles and Manifestation*, best-selling spiritual, magickal and paranormal author Embrosewyn Tazkuvel, reveals the secrets to summoning true magickal angels. And once called, how to use their awesome divine power to transform your compelling needs and desires into manifested reality.

Angel magick is the oldest, most powerful and least understood of all methods of magick. Ancient books of scripture from multiple religions tell of the marvelous power and miracles of angels. But the secrets of the true angel names, who they really are, their hierarchy, their stewardship responsibilities, their sigils, and how to successfully call them and have them work their divine magick for you, was lost to the world as a large part of it descended into the dark ages.

But a covenant was made by the Archangel Maeádael to the Adepts of Magick that as the people of the world evolved to a higher light the knowledge and power of angels would come again to the earth during the time of the Generation of Promise. That time is now. We are the Generation of Promise that has been foretold of for millennium. And all that was lost has been restored.

It doesn't matter what religion or path of enlightenment and empowerment that you travel: Wicca, Christianity, Pagan, Jewish, Buddhist, Occult, Muslim, Kabbalah, Vedic, something else or none at all. Nor does your preferred system of magick from Enochian, Thelemic, Gardnerian, Hermetic, to Tantric matter. Once you know the true names of the mighty angels, their unique sigils, and the simple but specific way to summon them, they will come and they will help you.

This revealing book of the ancient Celestine Light magick gives you immediate access to the divine powers of 14 Archangels, 136 Stewardship Angels, and hundreds of Specialty Angels that serve beneath them. Whether you are a novice or a magickal Adept you will find that when angels are on your side you manifest results that you never imagined possible except in your dreams.

The angel magick of Celestine Light is simple and direct without a lot of ritual, which makes it easy even for the novice to be able to quickly use it and gain benefit. While there is a place and importance to ritual in other types of magickal conjuring it is not necessary with angels. They are supernatural beings of unlimited power and awareness whose stewardship includes responding quickly to people in need who call upon them. You do not need elaborate rituals to get their attention.

If you are ready to have magick come alive in your life; if you are ready for real-life practical results that bring wisdom, happiness, health, love and abundance; if you are ready to unveil your life's purpose and unleash your own great potential, obtain the treasure that is this book. Call upon the magickal angels and they will come. But be prepared. When you summon angels, the magick happens and it is transformative. Your life will improve in ways big and small. But it will never be the same.

WORDS OF POWER AND TRANSFORMATION
101+ Magickal Words and Sigils of Celestine Light To Manifest Your Desires

Whatever you seek to achieve or change in your life, big or small, Celestine Light magickal words and sigils can help your sincere desires become reality.

Drawing from an ancient well of magickal power, the same divine source used by acclaimed sorcerers, witches and spiritual masters through the ages, the 101+ magickal words and sigils are revealed to the public for the very first time. They can create quick and often profound improvements in your life.

It doesn't matter what religion you follow or what you believe or do not believe. The magickal words and sigils are like mystical keys that open secret doors regardless of who holds the key. If you put the key in and turn it, the door will open and the magick will swirl around you!

From the beginner to the Adept, the Celestine Light words of power and sigils will expand your world and open up possibilities that may have seemed previously unachievable. Everything from something simple like finding a lost object, to something powerful like repelling a psychic or physical attack, to something of need such as greater income, to something life changing like finding your Soul Mate.

Some may wonder how a few spoken words combined with looking for just a moment at a peculiar image could have such immediate and often profound effects. The secret is these are ancient magick words of compelling power and the sigils are the embodiment of their magickal essence. Speaking or even thinking the words, or looking at or even picturing the sigil in your mind, rapidly draws angelic and magickal energies to you like iron to a magnet to fulfill the worthy purpose you desire.

This is a book of potent white magick of the light. Without a lot of training or ritual, it gives you the ability to overcome darkness threatening you from inside or out. For what is darkness except absence of the light? When light shines, darkness fades and disappears, not with a roar, but with a whimper.

Use the words and sigils to call in the magickal energies to transform and improve your life in every aspect. In this comprehensive book you will find activators to propel your personal growth, help you excel in school, succeed in your own business, or launch you to new heights in your profession. It will give you fast acting keys to improve your relationships, change your luck, revitalize your health, and develop and expand your psychic abilities.

Embrosewyn Tazkuvel is an Adept of the highest order in Celestine Light. After six decades of using magick and teaching it to others he is now sharing some of the secrets of what he knows with you. Knowledge that will instantly connect you to divine and powerful universal forces that with harmonic resonance, will unleash the magickal you!

Inside you will discover:

- 101 word combinations that call in magickal forces like a whirlwind of light.
- 177 magickal words in total.
- 101 sigils to go with each magickal word combination to amplify the magickal results you seek.
- 101 audio files you can listen to; helping you have perfect pronunciation of the Words of Power regardless of your native language. Available directly from the eBook and with a link in the paperback edition.

SOUL MATE AURAS
How to Find Your Soul Mate &
"Happily Ever After"

Find your own "Happily Ever After."
Experience the joy of finding your Soul Mate. Learn the simple secrets to discovering the love of your life!

Soul Mate Auras: How to Find Your Soul Mate & "Happily Ever After" uses dozens of full color pictures and the experience of 60 years of seeing auras, to give you the master keys to unlock the passageway to discovering your Soul Mate using the certainty of your auric connections. Every person has a unique aura and auric field generated by their seven energy centers. Find the person that you resonate strongly with on all seven energy centers and you'll find your Soul Mate!

You can sense and see auras, even if you never have!

In *Soul Mate Auras* full color eye and energy exercises will help you learn how to see and feel auras and how to use that ability to identify where in the great big world your Soul Mate is living. Once you are physically in the presence of your prospective Soul Mate, you will know how to use your aura to energetically confirm that they are the one. The same methods can be used to discover multiple people that are Twin Flames with you; not quite seven auric connection Soul Mates, but still deep and expansive connections to you on five to six energy centers.

Soul Mate Auras also includes an in-depth checklist method to determine if someone is your Twin Flame or Soul Mate.

This is a proven method of confirmation, not by using your aura, but by honestly and rationally evaluating your connections on all seven of your energy centers. This is an invaluable tool for anyone contemplating marriage or entering into a long-term committed relationship. It also serves as a useful second opinion confirmation for anyone that has used their aura to find their Soul Mate.

To help inspire and motivate you to create your own "happily ever after," Soul Mate Auras is richly accentuated with dozens of full color photos of loving couples along with profound quotes from famous to anonymous people about the wonder of Soul Mates.

Treat yourself to the reality of finding your Soul Mate or confirming the one that you have already found!

Secret Earth Series

INCEPTION
BOOK 1

Could it be possible that there is a man alive on the Earth today that has been here for two thousand years? How has he lived so long? And why? What secrets does he know? Can his knowledge save the Earth or is it doomed?

Continuing the epic historical saga begun in the *Oracles of Celestine Light*, but written as a novel rather than a chronicle, *Inception* unveils the life and adventures of Lazarus of Bethany and his powerful and mysterious sister Miriam of Magdala.

The first book of the Secret Earth series, *Inception*, reveals the hidden beginnings of the strange, secret life of Lazarus. From his comfortable position as the master of caravans to Egypt he is swept into a web of intrigue involving his enigmatic sister Miriam and a myriad of challenging dangers that never seem to end and spans both space and time.

Some say Miriam is an angel, while others are vehement that she is a witch. Lazarus learns the improbable truth about his sister, and along with twenty-three other courageous men and women, is endowed with the secrets of immortality. But he learns that living the secrets is not as easy as knowing them. And living them comes at a price; one that needs to be paid in unwavering courage, stained with blood, built with toil, and endured with millenniums of sacrifice, defending the Earth from all the horrors that might have been. *Inception* is just the beginning of their odyssey.

DESTINY
BOOK 2

In preparation, before beginning their training as immortal Guardians of the Earth, Lazarus of Bethany and his wife Hannah were asked to go on a short visit to a world in another dimension. "Just to look around a bit and get a feel for the differences," Lazarus's mysterious sister, Miriam of Magdala assured them.

She neglected to mention the ravenous monstrous birds, the ferocious fire-breathing dragons, the impossibly perfect people with sinister ulterior motives, and the fact that they would end up being naked almost all the time! And that was just the beginning of the challenges!

UNLEASH YOUR PSYCHIC POWERS

A Comprehensive 400 Page Guidebook

Unleash Your Psychic Powers is an entertaining, enlightening and educational resource for all levels of practitioners in the psychic, magickal and paranormal arts. It includes easy-to-follow, step-by-step instructions on how you can develop and enhance the full potential of dynamic psychic, magickal and paranormal powers in your own life.

Whether You Are A Novice Or An Adept

You will find valuable insight and guidance, based upon Embrosewyn's six decades of experience discovering and developing psychic and paranormal talents and unleashing the power of the magickal arts.

Twenty Psychic And Paranormal Abilities Are Explored

Including well known abilities such as Clairvoyance, Telekinesis, Telepathy, Lucid Dreaming, Precognition, Astral Projection and Faith Healing, plus, more obscure talents such as Channeling, Dowsing, and Automatic Handwriting.

In addition to helping you develop and master the psychic abilities that call to you, each of the twenty powers described are spiced with fascinating personal stories from the lives of Embrosewyn and others, to help you understand some of the real world consequences and benefits of using these formidable magickal and psychic talents. Paranormal abilities have saved Embrosewyn's life and the lives of his family members on multiple occasions. Learning to fully develop your own psychic and paranormal abilities may come in just as handy one day.

For anyone that is an active spirit medium, or uses any psychic abilities involving other-worldly beings, such as divination, channeling, or ghost hunting, the chapter on Psychic Self-defense is an extensive must read, covering low, medium and high risk threats, including everything from negative vortexes, to entities, energy vampires, ghosts, aliens and demons. Exorcism, and how to protect both people and property from unseen forces is also completely explained.

Filled with pictures and vivid descriptions of how you can bring forth and develop your own transcendental supernatural gifts, *Unleash Your Psychic Powers* should be in the library of every serious student of the psychic, magickal, paranormal and supernatural.

Everyone has psychic and paranormal abilities. It is your birthright! You were born with them!

Within this book you'll learn how to unlock and unleash your astounding supernatural potential and the amazing things you can do with your powers once they are free!

PSYCHIC SELF DEFENSE

A Complete Guide to Protecting Yourself Against Psychic & Paranormal Attack (and just plain irksome people)

Felt a negative energy come over you for no apparent reason when you are near someone or around certain places? Had a curse hurled at you? Spooked by a ghost in a building? Imperiled by demonic forces? Being drained and discombobulated by an energy vampire? Or, do you encounter more mundane but still disruptive negative energies like an over demanding boss, the local bully, hurtful gossip, a physically or mentally abusive spouse, or life in a dangerous neighborhood threatened by thieves and violence? Whatever your source of negative energy, danger or threat, you'll find effective, proven, psychic and magickal countermeasures within this book.

Psychic Self Defense draws upon Embrosewyn's six decades of personal experience using psychic abilities and magickal defenses to thwart, counter and send back to sender, any and all hostile paranormal threats. Everything from unsupportive and dismissive family and friends, to ghosts, demons and exorcisms. The same practical and easy to learn Magickal techniques can be mastered by anyone serious enough to give it some time and practice, and can aid you immensely with a host of material world challenges as well.

17 psychic and paranormal threats are covered with exact, effective counter measures, including many real life examples from Embrosewyn's comprehensive personal experiences with the paranormal, devising what works and what doesn't from hard won trial and error.

Whether you are a medium needing to keep foul spirits away, or simply someone desiring to know that you, your family and property are safe and protected, you will find the means to insure peace and security with the proven methods outlined in *Psychic Self Defense*

You will learn how to:
- Create your own Magick spells tailored to your particular situation and need
- Call upon specific angels to aid you
- Create Crystal Energy Shields
- Protect yourself when in a channeling or spirit medium trance
- Use your Aura to create ASP's (Auric Shields of Power)
- Empower Wards for protection against specific threats
- Recognize and counter Energy Vampires
- Cleanse a home of negative energy
- Cut negative energy cords to disharmonious people
- Counter Black Magick
- Detect alien presence
- Banish malicious entities or demons

Though dealing with numerous and sometimes dangerous other-worldly and material world threats, the entire approach of this book is from a position of personal empowerment, no fear, and divine white light. Whether you are religious or an atheist, an experienced practitioner of the psychic and magickal arts or a neophyte, someone living in a haunted house or just an employee wanting to have a nicer boss, there will be hundreds of ways you can use the information in this book to help you in your life. And you will learn to do it in ways that are uplifting and empowering, producing results that are peaceful, safe and harmonious.

Psychic Self Defense is also available as an AUDIO BOOK.

22 STEPS TO THE LIGHT OF YOUR SOUL

A Treasured Book That Will Help You Unleash The Greatness Within

What would it be like if you could reach through space and time to query the accumulated wisdom of the ages and get an answer? *22 Steps to the Light of Your Soul,* reveals such treasured insights, eloquently expounding upon the foundational principles of 22 timeless subjects of universal interest and appeal, to help each reader grow and expand into their fullest potential.

In a thought-provoking, poetic writing style, answers to questions we all ponder upon, such as love, happiness, success and friendship, are explored and illuminated in short, concise chapters, perfect for a thought to ponder through the day or contemplate as your eyes close for sleep.

Each paragraph tells a story and virtually every sentence could stand alone as an inspiring quote on your wall.

These are the 22 steps of the Light of Your Soul
Step 1: The Purpose of Life
Step 2: Balance
Step 3: Character
Step 4: Habits
Step 5: Friendship
Step 6: True Love
Step 7: Marriage
Step 8: Children
Step 9: Happiness
Step 10: Play & Relaxation
Step 11: Health
Step 12: Success
Step 13: Knowledge
Step 14: Passion & Serenity
Step 15: Imagination & Vision
Step 16: Creativity & Art

Step 17: Adversity
Step 18: Respect
Step 19: Freedom & Responsibility
Step 20: Stewardship
Step 21: Faith
Step 22: Love Yourself - the Alpha and the Omega

ALSO AVAILABLE AS AN AUDIO BOOK! You can listen as you commute to work or travel on vacation, or even listen and read together!

LOVE YOURSELF
The Secret Key to Transforming Your Life

Loving yourself is all about energy

As humans we devote a great deal of our energy through our time, thoughts and emotions to love. We read about it, watch movies and shows about it, dream about it, hope for it to bless our lives, feel like something critically important is lacking when it doesn't, and at the very least keep a sharp eye out for it when its missing.

Too often we look to someone else to fulfill our love and crash and burn when relationships end, or fail to live up to our fantasies of what we thought they should be. When we seek love from another person or source greater than the love we give to ourselves, we set ourselves up to an inevitable hard landing when the other person or source ceases to provide the level of fulfillment we desire.

Loving yourself is a precious gift from you to you. It is an incredibly powerful energy that not only enhances your ability to give love more fully to others, it also creates a positive energy of expanding reverberation that brings more love, friendship and appreciation to you from all directions. It is the inner light that illuminates your life empowering you to create the kind of life you desire and dream.

The relationship you have with yourself is the most important one in your life. Happiness will forever be fleeting if you do not have peace, respect and love for yourself. It's not selfish. It's not vain. It is in fact the key to transforming your life. Inward reflection and appreciation will open up clearer channels to the divine. Relationships with everyone will be enhanced as your relationship with yourself expands and is uplifted.

All other relationships are only mirrors of the one you have within. As you love yourself, are kind to yourself, respect yourself, so too will you be able to give those and so many other good qualities to others in equal measure to that which you give to yourself.

This is a short, but very sweet book to help you discover your inner glow of love. Within its covers are two great keys you will find no other place. These two keys will proactively bring you to the serenity of self-love regardless of whether you are currently near or far from that place of peace.

Are you familiar with the infinity symbol? It looks pretty much like the number 8 turned on its side. As love for yourself should be now and forever, in the last chapter you will find 88 reasons why loving yourself is vitally important to your joy, personal growth and expansion, and the happiness of everyone whose lives you touch. Most people have never considered that there could be a list that long just about loving yourself! But with each short phrase you read your mind begins to understand to a greater depth how important loving yourself is for all aspects of your life and relationships. As your mind understands your life follows.

This book leaves you with a special gift Inside you'll find two short, but very valuable multimedia flash presentations. One is entitled "Forgive Yourself". The other is "Love Yourself" These are not normal flash presentations. They are self-hypnosis, positive affirmations that will rapidly help you achieve greater self-love and more fulfilling love-filled realities in your life. As soft repetitive music plays in the background, images reinforcing the theme will flash by on your screen about three per second, accompanied by short phrases superimposed on a portion of the image. In a quick 7-10 minute session, sitting at home in front of your computer, you will find the flash presentations buoy and motivate you. Repeat them twice a day for several days and you will find they are transformative.

Special Bonus: *Love Yourself* is ALSO AVAILABLE AS AN AUDIO BOOK! This allows you to listen and read at the same time!

ORACLES OF CELESTINE LIGHT
Complete Trilogy Of Genesis, Nexus & Vivus

Once in a lifetime comes a book that can dramatically change your life for the better - forever. This is it!

WHAT WAS LOST...HAS BEEN FOUND

This is the complete 808 page trilogy of the Celestine books of Light: Genesis, Nexus and Vivus.

The controversial *Oracles of Celestine Light*, is a portal in time to the days of Yeshua of Nazareth, over 2000 years ago, revealed in fulfilling detail to the world by the reclusive Embrosewyn Tazkuvel. It includes 155 chapters of sacred wisdom, miracles and mysteries revealing life-changing knowledge about health, longevity, happiness and spiritual expansion that reverberates into your life today.

Learn the startling, never before understood truth:

About aliens, other dimensions, Atlantis, Adam & Eve, the Garden of Eden, Noah and the ark, giants, the empowerment of women, dreams, angels, Yeshua of Nazareth (Jesus), his crucifixion & resurrection, his wife Miriam of Magdala (Mary Magdala), Yudas Iscariot (Judas), the afterlife, reincarnation, energy vortexes, witches, magic, miracles, paranormal abilities, and you!

The Oracles of Celestine Light turns accepted religious history and traditional teachings on their head. But page by page, it makes more sense than anything you´ve ever read and shares simple yet profound truths to make your life better today and help you to understand and unleash your miraculous potential.

The *Oracles of Celestine Light* explains who you are, why you are here, and your divine destiny. It is a must-read for anyone interested in spirituality, personal growth and thought-provoking answers to the unknown.

"You are a child of God, a Child of Light, literally a priceless son or daughter of divinity. Even through the fog of mortal upheavals and the tumults and tribulations, always remember you are still a child of God and shall inherit joy and kingdoms beyond measure, as you remain true to your light." Genesis 11:99

Psychic Awakening Series
CLAIRVOYANCE

Would it be helpful if you could gain hidden knowledge about a person, place, thing, event, or concept, not by any of your five physical senses, but with visions and "knowing?"
Are you ready to supercharge your intuition? *Clairvoyance*, takes you on a quest of self-discovery and personal empowerment, helping you unlock this potent ESP ability in your life. It includes riveting stories from Embrosewyn's six decades of psychic and paranormal adventures, plus fascinating accounts of others as they discovered and cultivated their supernatural abilities.

Clearly written, step-by-step practice exercises will help you to expand and benefit from your own psychic and clairvoyant abilities. This can make a HUGE improvement in your relationships, career and creativity. As Embrosewyn has proven from over twenty years helping thousands of students to find and develop their psychic and paranormal abilities, EVERYONE, has one or more supernatural gifts. *Clairvoyance* will help you discover and unleash yours!

If you are interested in helping yourself to achieve more happiness, better health, greater knowledge, increased wealth and a deeper spirituality, unlocking your power of clairvoyance can be the key. Hidden knowledge revealed becomes paths unseen unveiled.

Unleashing your psychic gifts does more than just give you advantage in life challenges. It is a safe, ethical, even spiritual and essential part of you that makes you whole, once you accept that you have these special psychic abilities and begin to use them.

TELEKINESIS

Easy, comprehensive guide for anyone wanting to develop the supernatural ability of Telekinesis

Telekinesis, also known as psychokinesis, is the ability to move or influence the properties of objects without physical contact. Typically it is ascribed as a power of the mind. But as Embrosewyn explains, based upon his sixty years of personal experience, the actual physical force that moves and influences objects emanates from a person's auric field. It initiates with a mental thought, but the secret to the power is in your aura!

Telekinesis is the second book in the Psychic Awakening series by popular paranormal writer Embrosewyn Tazkuvel. The series was specifically created to offer short, inexpensive, information filled handbooks to help you quickly learn and develop specific psychic and paranormal abilities.

Clearly written, *Telekinesis* is filled with step-by-step practice exercises and training techniques proven to help you unlock this formidable paranormal ability. Spiced with riveting accounts of real-life psychic experiences and paranormal adventures, you'll be entertained while you learn. But along the way you will begin to unleash the potent power of Telekinesis in your own life!

As Embrosewyn has proven from over twenty years helping thousands of students to find and develop their psychic and paranormal abilities. EVERYONE, has one or more supernatural gifts. Is Telekinesis one of yours? Perhaps it's time to find out.

DREAMS

Awaken in the world of your sleep

In *Dreams*, the third book of the Psychic awakening series, renowned psychic/paranormal practitioner Embrosewyn Tazkuvel reveals some of his personal experiences with the transformational effect of dreams, while sharing time-tested techniques and insights that will help you unlock the power of your own night travels.

Lucid Dreaming

An expanded section on Lucid Dreaming gives you proven methods to induce and develop your innate ability to control your dreams. It explores the astonishing hidden world of your dream state that can reveal higher knowledge, greatly boost your creativity, improve your memory, and help you solve vexing problems of everyday life that previously seemed to have no solution.

Nine Types of Dreams

Detailing the nine types of dreams will help you to understand which dreams are irrelevant and which you should pay close attention to, especially when they reoccur. You'll gain insight into how to interpret the various types of dreams to understand which are warnings and which are gems of inspiration that can change your life from the moment you awaken and begin to act upon that which you dreamed.

Become the master of your dreams

Sleeping and dreaming are a part of your daily life that cumulatively accounts for dozens of years of your total life. It is a valuable time of far more than just rest. Become the master of your dreams and your entire life can become more than you ever imagined possible. Your dreams are the secret key to your future.

EMBROSEWYN'S

Magickal Gems

Enchanted Jewelry, Gems & Tools

www.magickalgems.com

Additional Services Offered by Embrosewyn

I am honored to be able to be of further service to you by offering multiple paranormal abilities for your enlightenment and life assistance. On a limited basis as my time allows I can:

- discover your Soul Name and the meaning and powers of the sounds

- custom craft and imbue enchantments upon a piece of your jewelry for a wide beneficial range of purposes

- discover the name of your Guardian Angel

- have an in-depth psychic consultation and Insight Card reading with you via a Skype video call.

My wife Sumara can also create a beautiful piece of collage art on 20"x30" internally framed canvas, representing all of the meanings and powers of the sounds of your Soul Name.

If you are interested in learning more about any of these additional services please visit my website: *www.embrosewyn.com* and click on the link at the top for SERVICES.

If you would like to purchase enchanted jewelry or gemstones for specific purposes such as love, health, good fortune, or psychic protection please visit my website: *www.magickalgems.com.*

For great info on a wide variety of psychic, paranormal and magick subjects, please visit my YouTube Channel, *Esoteric Mystery*

School with Embrosewyn Tazkuvel.

NOTES

Lightning Source UK Ltd.
Milton Keynes UK
UKHW021014030620
364334UK00007B/92